GOLF
MASTER CLASSES

GOLF MASTER CLASSES

A Champion's Guide To Better Golf

PETER ALLISS
with Michael Hobbs

Macdonald
Queen Anne Press

A QUEEN ANNE PRESS BOOK

© Peter Alliss and Michael Hobbs 1986, 1989

First published in Great Britain by Orbis Publishing Limited, London, 1986

This edition published in 1989 by
Queen Anne Press, a division of
Macdonald & Co (Publishers) Ltd
Orbit House
1 New Fetter Lane
London
EC4A 1AR

A member of Maxwell Macmillan Pergamon Publishing Corporation

1st reprint, May 1990
2nd reprint, February 1991

Cover photograph by Peter Dazeley

British Library Cataloguing Publishing Data
Alliss, Peter, *1931-*
   Golf master classes: a champion's guide to better
   golf
   I. Title II. Hobbs, Michael, *1934-*
   796.352

   ISBN 0-356-17849-8

   Printed and bound in Italy by Graphicom

CONTENTS

PREFACE

Many of the books on playing golf that have been published over the last hundred years or so have really been concerned with the question of how the golf club should be swung on full shots. Undoubtedly, it is a very important part of the game and one that I hope I have covered fully in this book, but there is more to golf than that. A golfer meets many situations throughout his or her playing days and needs particular shots to match each. One does not just need to know how to get out of a bunker, for instance, but should have a whole range of bunker shots for different situations depending on the lie of the ball and the conditions. You do not only have to be able to hit a long ball but you also have to know when *not* to do so, and also how to drive safely.

In this book I've tried to cover the ground that is so often overlooked. In doing so, I've drawn not just on my own expertise but also from what I've learned while playing with, talking to, or watching all the greats of the last thirty and more years.

From these experiences, one of the things I have learned is that there is seldom one right way of doing anything in golf. Although there are a few basic rules that all good players follow, consciously or unconsciously, they vary very widely indeed within them.

Because golf is a complex game, it requires a variety of skills, and there is no magic formula for improving your game. If there was, you could be sure that someone would have discovered it years ago! However, there is one simple piece of advice, which can be guaranteed to help you improve. That is, know yourself. Learn to see your game as it really is. Question what you are doing and discover how to look at your game objectively.

With that in mind I'd like you to relate everything that you read in the following pages to an honest appraisal of your game. For each particular shot look at your average result with it. Think, for instance, 'Do I ever hit a long iron well?' If your answer is, 'Yes, but only a few times a year,' then accept that you have two alternatives: work on this part of your game, hoping to become competent, or give up expecting much from these clubs, and learn to substitute something else.

There is another word that I want to whisper in your ear, and that is the dread sound, 'practice'. Only a small part of what I have to say throughout this book can be applied without practice and experiment. So many club golfers never hit a practice ball, and so many of the rest practise in the wrong ways, all because so few enjoy the experience. But I hope that I can persuade you that practice can be fun, and not the grinding, stupefying regime it is often thought to be.

One word on the style of this book. There are hosts of left-handers around. I have therefore tried to avoid the right-hand bias as far as possible, and throughout have used words such as 'front', 'back', 'top', 'bottom', 'leading' and 'trailing' for the 'left' and 'right' that are no easier to understand for right-handers but which are an obstacle, even if a minor one, for left-handers.

Finally, this book is aimed at those for whom golf is already an established part of their lives, and who are looking for ways of improving their game. You may not be an advanced golfer now; I hope you will be, though, by the time you get to the end, and, even if you do not scale the heights, I trust that you will find that you have made your game more pleasurable.

ACKNOWLEDGE-MENTS

Various people have helped in making this book, many of whom must remain anonymous because their contributions were made subtly and indirectly over the years. I am thinking of my fellow golfers, professional and amateur, who have influenced me and my game. My thanks go to them for all their tips and advice, generously given throughout my golfing career, and to all those people I have listened to, argued with, and learned from.

Specifically, my thanks go to three people who have made a direct and creative contribution to the production of the book. Ken Lewis' imaginative and illuminating drawings add so much to the 'feel' of this volume. How well he captures the 'mental' picture of the game.

Peter Dazeley is one of a very small band of specialized photographers whose work I have long admired. He always manages to capture the exact mood of the moment, whether it be a full blooded drive, or the most delicate of chip shots.

My thanks also go to Michael Hobbs, with whom I have enjoyed working on this as on numerous other occasions. We have developed a relationship where we shout quite often at each other but still manage to make it all work. Thank you, Michael, for all your hard labours, and perhaps most of all for your enthusiasm.

Finally, I must record my gratitude to Rex Thompson for his advice on various matters affecting golf clubs, including maintenance and repair, and to the London Kosaido Golf Club for letting us photograph on their course.

Grip fast, stand with your left leg first not farr;
Incline your back and shoulders, but bewarre
You raise them not when back the club you bring;
Make all the motion with your bodies swinge
And shoulders, holding still the muscles bent;
Play slowly first till you the way have learnt.
At such lenth hold the club as fits your strenth
The lighter head requires the longer lenth
That circle wherein moves your club and hands
At forty-five degree from the horizon stands.
When at on stroak to effecuat you dispaire
Seek only 'gainst the next it to prepare

From the diary of Thomas Kincaid, 1688

REVISION
COURSE

You may have been playing for years, and feel that the fundamentals of golf are so much part of your game that you do not need to think about them. If that is the case, beware; it's amazing just how often experienced players lose out on their game because of some basic fault, or how often they can pick up a new tip that will make that important difference.

All the great and good players regularly examine the basics. Jones and Nicklaus, for example, always prepared for a new season by getting someone they felt really knew their games to look them over – Nicklaus still does today.

They knew, or know, that there's a great deal the player can't see for himself. Both the eye and what you feel can be wrong. Great players have, without knowing it, come to let little faults creep into their positioning, their swing or their aim. If this can happen even to outstanding players, it is, of course, much more common amongst club golfers. However, there are various checks that you can carry out yourself.

THE GRIP

Together with how you stand to the ball and aim, how you hold the club is one of the most basic elements of playing golf well. Yet many people seem to play golf with some very strange grips indeed. Perhaps the top hand is turned so that the back of the hand is nowhere near facing the target line, or the palm of the bottom hand is askew. I do see people able to play quite well with both of these basic alignments utterly wrong, but they are making the game more difficult for themselves, and when they are off form can play appallingly badly. And not only does a bad grip make the game much more difficult than it need be, it stops you playing better than you could, even when things are going well.

Many's the time I've given lessons where my pupil has said: 'I'll do whatever you tell me, but please don't make me change my grip.' One can't do much for him if that's his attitude. Indeed, the grip certainly is very personal, being the point of physical focus, and a change of, let's say, a quarter of an inch can make the whole feel of the golf swing utterly different, but it will also affect more than the feel. My own grip is, I assure you, utterly orthodox, although there have been players who have diverted from this straight and narrow path with some success. But they have not usually been Champions, though the left hand grips of Trevino, Locke and Thomson are exceptional in their different ways.

Let's think for a moment about the function of a good grip. It really must allow you to be able to do all of the following:

1 Keep the clubface in a constant relationship with the target line. Obviously it won't be square all the time because your body will be turning on the backswing and your arms will be swinging on a different axis. Nevertheless, that clubface will start off more or less square to the target, gradually open till the clubhead is parallel to the target line at the top of the swing and then, without any manipulation with the hands, return on line to target at the moment of impact. In other

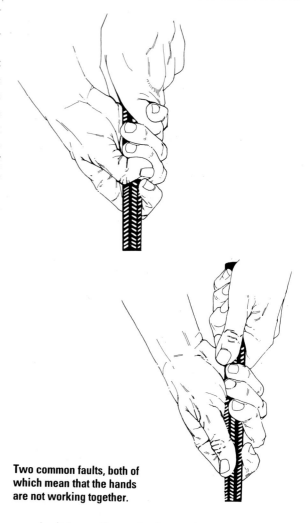

Two common faults, both of which mean that the hands are not working together.

words, it turns through ninety degrees, and then back again.

2 Allow your wrists first to break and later to cock fully in such a way that they both do so in unison. Only if this is so will you be able to release fully through the ball.

3 Keep all those parts of both hands and fingers which started off in contact with your club grip in unchanged position during the back- and down-swing, at impact and even in the follow-through. Henry Cotton always preached that a golfer with a sound grip should be able to hit a succession of practice shots without needing to regrip. As with so much else that Henry had to say about our game, I am in full agreement with his view.

If you're still in doubt, having tried this experiment, just have a close look at your hands. Feel the texture of the skin. Is it smooth, even delicate? It is? Excellent! Unless you're playing very little golf indeed, this is a good indication that the clubshaft is not moving in your hands. If it is, then callouses form quickly. Your hands will also quickly get sore and then blistered once you've hit thirty or so balls on your club's practice ground or at a driving range.

So, the aim of a good grip is to control the clubhead. How, then, to achieve it? The grip will not be exactly the same for everyone, as small variations are, of course, caused by the length of the fingers and width of the palm. However, the experts are agreed as to where the club should lie across the bottom hand. This is entirely in the fingers. The shaft should run slightly on the diagonal from the base of the little finger (if you have a ten-fingered grip on the club) and finish in the crook of the forefinger, tight into the joint.

Exactly the same will apply to your top hand. True, it may feel to be slightly more in the palm but this really isn't so. Because the shaft is thicker at the top, rather more of your palm will touch your club's grip – and that's all.

For the top hand, there are two exceptions, however. Most good swingers of a golf club fear a hook more than a slice. Jack Nicklaus, for example who from his teenage days has always tried to play with fade, has nevertheless hit some very destructive hooks in his time. Roberto de Vicenzo, one of the very best strikers and swingers I've

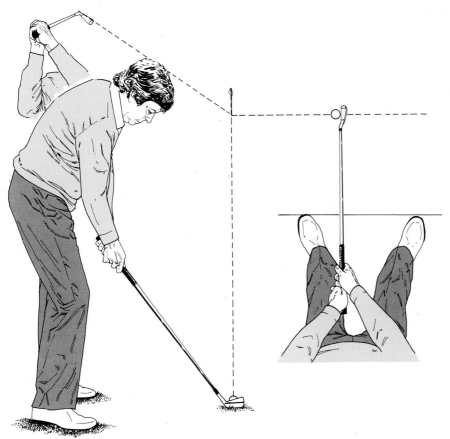

Providing you have the correct address position, a good grip will enable you to start with the clubface square to the target, opening until it is parallel to the target line at the top of the backswing.

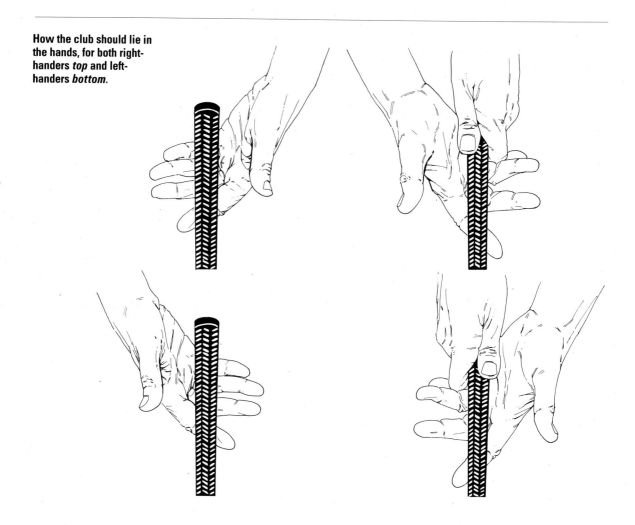

How the club should lie in the hands, for both right-handers *top* and left-handers *bottom*.

seen, aimed to draw the ball slightly – but this was just a slight curl towards the end of flight. He, too, was afraid of hooking. Finally, there is the classic example of Ben Hogan. For his height and weight, he was a tremendously long hitter but achieved a good deal of this length from the extra run that a drawn shot gets from skipping along the fairway. All of these players, to help them avoid hooking, adopted a top hand grip with the shaft running much more in the palm. However, this is only a matter of degree. Instead of the club resting at the base of the little finger, the butt is positioned halfway between here and the heel of the hand. Hogan, of course was eventually in a different category from all the other players of his day and was able to work the ball both ways the amount he wanted.

The other exception is that this is one of the few areas of golf where the women's game differs from the men's. Less strength in the hands has led many of the top players to have a top hand position where three or even more knuckles are showing. A strong woman such as the great JoAnne Carner plays with a conventional male grip, but others like Judy Rankin and Nancy Lopez, get more of the heel of the hand facing the target as they find it gives them a stronger feel. Although almost without exception the best modern men do not use this grip, if you go further back in time you can come across examples in plenty, Gene Sarazen and the Whitcombe brothers being the most notable ones.

However, I don't recommend it for men except as a last resort. I believe that though it can work, you need to be in constant practice to make up for the fact that you're making the game more difficult for yourself.

Many players ask how tightly they should hold the club. This is the wrong way of looking at it. The grip should never be *tight*. It may, and should, however, be *firm*. Believe me, there's a world of difference.

However, that said, there has been a world of difference in just how firmly some great players have held the club. There is no doubt at all that Hogan, Palmer, Watson and Nicklaus do not have light, delicate grips. Palmer, in particular, gives

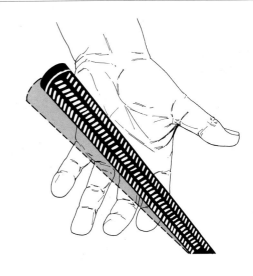

Above: Hogan's grip. The butt is closer to the heel of the hand.

Below: The overlapping or Vardon grip *left,* and the interlocking grip.

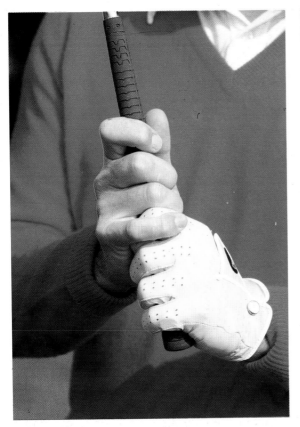

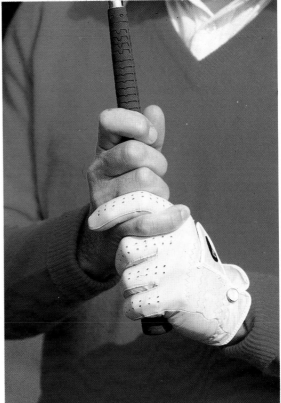

one the feeling that just no one on earth could wrest that club from his grasp. All are pretty strong men anyway. The key thing about them is that they can grip firmly with their fingers, without arm, shoulder and neck muscles tightening up in sympathy. For them a very firm grip is essential, but it must be achieved through finger strength alone. This is why Henry Cotton always taught golfers to have strong fingers and to squeeze squash balls and hit against car tyres or in the rough in order to develop this strength. But other great players have different views.

Grip pressure

Let me take the great Australian, Peter Thomson, as the first example. Until the achievements of Tom Watson, no one had so dominated the British Open over a period of years. Thomson's general belief was that a 'light, tender sensitive touch is worth a ton of brawn'. Obviously, this extended to the grip. Here, he felt that the club should be held only firmly enough for you to move it from the ground. He liked to feel the heaviness of the clubhead and believed that the grip progressively tightened through the swing automatically, until it was at its firmest at impact with the ball.

Bobby Locke went even further. He felt that this firming-up of the grip should be avoided even in the hitting area, believing that if the grip tightened, then the swing path might well be affected for the worse. In a nutshell, his opinion was that throughout the swing the club should be held only firmly enough to prevent it actually falling out of the hands.

Sam Snead, though far more powerful a golfer than either Thomson or Locke (either of whom amply punched his weight), felt much the same way. He believed that grip pressure should be much like holding a knife and fork. A light grip enables the golfer to feel the clubhead. A tight grip enables the golfer to feel the shaft, but not the head.

Walter Hagen, the source of more golf stories than any other player in golfing history, at a crucial point in a tournament once told his opponent to 'roll down your sleeves. They'll see your muscles bulging.' Well, I'm sure this could offend against normal golfing etiquette and, had not all been bewitched by his charm, might have earned him a bloodied nose. But the message is clear: 'Hold the club lightly.'

So too, the world's greatest young golfer, Seve Ballesteros: he teaches, 'You must never see your forearm muscles swelling.' Like Snead, he's a player of immense power and, I believe, better than any either of his contemporaries or of his predecessors combines immense power with delicacy of touch.

As regards my own game, I have a medium grip pressure. By this I mean that I have the feeling of the club being very firmly held by the fingers but equally can always feel the weight of the clubhead; I also always want to feel where it is and how it is aimed throughout my swing. I try to avoid all tension in the forearms in the swing.

There is, I think, a message here. Great players can be split – rather imperfectly – into two distinct groups. There are those who hit full out and, of course, are also very good putters. Like Palmer and Nicklaus, say, they do tend to be much less effective at half shots and delicate pitch shots into the greens. The other extreme are champions such as Thomson and Locke, relatively 'underpowered' but more blessed with that magic feel in the finger tips when in the 50 to 80 yard range.

Very few have straddled the boundary. Indeed my only real candidates would be Sam Snead and Seve Ballesteros, both very long off the tee, both equally capable of improvising and possessed with the feel for distance, the look of the shot, shape of ground and the run of a ball.

I shall have to leave it up to you to decide which group you belong to. Experiment on the practice ground and during practice rounds. On an average sort of day, do you do better holding the club firmly or gently?

No, I would agree with you, it's not a simple answer. Nothing in golf ever is.

BALL DISTANCE

It is important for the ball to be the right distance from the body in the stance for a full shot, as the results of this being incorrect are severe. Basically, if the ball is too far away, the player has to reach out for it. He is almost bound to swing too flat and will be less than ideally balanced because the weight of his upper body begins to shift too soon on to his toes. He has a built-in crouch and this is one of the main reasons for not being able to 'stand tall'.

If the ball is too close, on the other hand, the player becomes cramped. He has to lift the club upwards rather than swing back and turn, and will chop down too steeply at and across the ball. This leads to loss of power, especially on the wooden club shots, and a slicing action across the ball. He'll hit a lot of shots off the toe and lose 30 per cent of potential power.

Getting the correct distance is not a matter of measuring by feet and inches. The procedure is, however, simple: if we do a few things right in our posture, the ball should be where the club meets the ground. Make sure your knees are relaxed and slightly flexed, your behind a touch out, your back upright and your arms hanging freely. The 'freely hanging arms' have often been mentioned in golf instruction writing but there's more to it than that. After all, it's common sense that if you let your arms hang totally freely while holding a golf club, it will merely dangle between your legs, pendulum-fashion. Here, then, is the control or gimmick, you need.

If your upper arms are well clear of your chest, you are too far away from the ball. If your elbows and, even worse, your forearms seem likely to brush against your stomach, you are too close.

Having got these things adjusted to your satisfaction, keep the spine straight and bend from the waist until your clubhead just touches the ground. That's where the ball should be.

Standing too far from the ball *left* produces too flat a swing, while standing too close results in an upward lift of the club.

Right: One way of finding the right position: the knees are flexed, backside out a little, back upright, and the arms free but not dangling. Then bend from the waist until the clubhead touches the ground, and that's where the ball should be.

Below: The correct position.

Below: The ideal set-up for a long iron.

TAKING AIM

Many club golfers reach their ball, put the clubhead behind it, begin fiddling with the stance and *only then* look up to see where they're going.

This is just about the exact reverse order of what should actually happen. Start viewing your shot while you walk towards your ball. Visualize a straight line from your ball to the target – the flag or some point down the fairway. It's also very useful to pick a feature much nearer to your ball, two or three feet away, which lies on your target line. Having selected which club will get you to the target, you can then think solely of hitting the ball through the daisy, twig, leaf, tuft of grass or whatever that you've chosen.

Next, align both your clubface and body with the target, the clubface first. I suggest you settle into a habit of holding the club with one hand only at this point. Add the other when you've completed the rest of the set-up. Bernhard Langer, for example, starts with his right hand and foot. He's a good man to study because he is so deliberate in taking aim.

I don't think it matters very much which hand you decide to use. Jack Nicklaus, for instance, follows what used to be taught in my young days and starts off with the top hand, his left. Seve Ballesteros does precisely the reverse, and follows the drill, right hand, body alignment, left hand, swing.

Having done this, get your shoulders and hips parallel with target line. Then line up the forearms; check this very carefully. So many golfers reach *round* when they set their bottom hand on the club rather than *under*, thus swinging the shoulders round rather than tilting slighty down. Finally, your feet should be at approximately shoulder width. It's a better fault to have them somewhat too close together than too far apart as this helps stimulate free leg action and frees the arms. A line drawn from toe to toe should also be parallel with the target line. Your thighs and knees should then automatically fall into place.

You will probably find this set-up easier to do if you place your rear foot in position first. The whole procedure will result in the standard

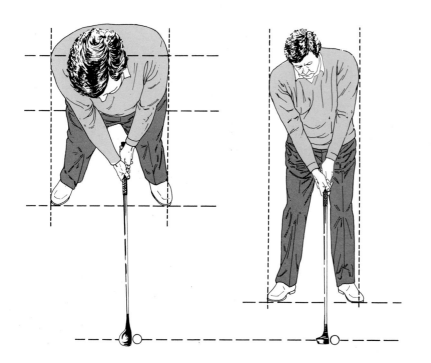

Toes, hips and shoulders should all be parallel with the target line.

'square' set-up in which everything is parallel to the target line. You'll notice, however, that a very high proportion of professionals set up slightly 'open'. This means that the leading foot is withdrawn from the ball by a couple of inches or so, also causing the hip to follow suit. They find this helps to begin the downswing with the legs leading and to clear the leading hip more easily. Note, however, that arms and shoulders must keep that side-on position.

A 'shut' position works for very few really good players, though Bobby Locke, who drew the ball some 30 or 40 yards through the air, was an exception. But Locke was a genius, an eccentric in nearly everything he did in golf. Also, I do not recommend you try a shut stance as a cure for slicing: it will tend to shorten your backswing and make it more difficult than ever for you to swing through the ball with full freedom, both of which make slicing even more likely. You can be the world's worst slicer even though you have a very strong hooker's grip.

THE BACKSWING

This is all the movements that take place after you've gripped the club and perhaps had a waggle or two until the transition to the downswing.

Many players believe that the way the club is moved during the first foot or two of the back-

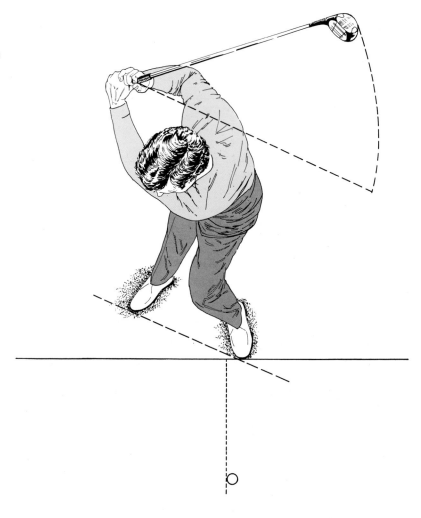

The 'shut' position favoured by Bobby Locke. This position usually shortens the backswing.

swing determines the success or failure of the shot. Certainly, a bad take-away usually produces a bad shot – unfortunately, a good take-away doesn't necessarily produce a good one.

Jack Nicklaus once pointed out to me that a golfer has mental control over his actions only before he begins the movement and for the early part of the backswing. And this only applies if that backswing is slow.

A friend of mine and a great golfing enthusiast, the late Raymond Oppenheimer, believed that what came immediately before was the most vital element in the whole swing. The whole movement, he said, ought to be kicked off by a forward press. My own key was to try to *start* back slowly and be slow and rhythmic especially for the first two or three inches.

Of course, there's never just one way of doing something in golf, but the aim is to stay easy and relaxed. On TV, you can see how players tackle this problem. Some repeatedly adjust their grips or waggle many times. Fuzzy Zoeller, the 1984 US Open Champion, has the habit of bouncing the clubhead up and down behind the ball. Nicklaus nowadays makes a slight forward press, though for many years he just strengthened his grip at the last moment. He also turns his head away from the ball as if concentrating on seeing it only from his left eye. Gary Player starts with a movement of the right knee towards the ball, while others ease their whole body just an inch or so towards the target. Most players try to have a feeling of 'liveliness' in the legs.

A slight forward movement in the knees will work for most players. Then feel those knees beginning the take-away. It seems quite logical really – we are going to want the legs to lead the downswing so they should come first right through the swing.

Others think more in terms of a movement with either hip while Seve Ballesteros likes to have his left knee, shoulder and hip beginning to turn in one piece.

Note, however, that not many great players, if indeed any, recommend that the hands alone should start things off. It has been proved the more the hands dominate at the start of the backswing, the more they will tend to come in too early in the downswing. As Ben Hogan once said: 'The golf swing is sort of like a Western movie. Set it up so the good guys can take over. Then the bad ones can't.'

To the top

Let's get the question of when to break the wrists out of the way first. To some extent it can be a matter of personal preference. I played very well for a time in 1958 breaking the wrists early and thinking of moving the clubhead away first. It brought me the Italian, Spanish and Portuguese Opens in three weeks and I wished the season would never end. Alas, the following year the magic formula no longer worked. Johnny Miller and Tom Watson regularly break early.

At the other end of the scale, Jack Nicklaus has always insisted that almost all the turning movement should be completed before the wrist break. He feels this at least helps to make sure that the shoulders turn fully.

This is probably the safer line to take unless you find it really doesn't suit you. With an early wrist break, there's more danger that the swing will become rather a straight up-and-down affair with restricted turn. Beware of picking up the club and nipping at the ball with no great width to your backswing.

Speed of backswing

There's a remarkable difference in the total time players take to make a swing. The average is about $1\frac{1}{2}$ seconds. Nicklaus, however, stretches it to 2 seconds, and very fast swingers – say in the Mark James and Brian Waites mould (who both have rather short backswings) – use up about 1 second. Virtually all this difference is accounted for by the different speed of backswing.

Brian Waites and another quick swinger, Charlie Ward, are amongst the most accurate drivers I've seen. They can swing back fast and still preserve good rhythm. Can you? I venture to

think not. For the majority of good players the backswing should be seen as a way of getting the club back into position to begin the downswing with everything balanced and rhythmic. It should be a rather quiet movement up to a position where you feel poised to swing down and through the ball. Always remember that old truism: you don't hit the ball with your backswing.

THE DOWNSWING

It has often been claimed that a good backswing leads to a good downswing. The whole process, it is felt, is as inevitable as night following day. But is it really?

Left: **Quarter of the way up the backswing.**

Below: **Trevino takes the club away from his body, but gets it back on line from ball to target in the hitting area.**

Several very superior players spring to mind with backswings that are highly unorthodox. Examples include the great Irish amateur James Bruen, Miller Barber (he has so many changes of direction one feels he needs a map to get back to the ball), once a putt or so away from winning the US Open and currently one of the best players on the US Senior Tour, and another American Gay Brewer, of the double loop. One of the all-time greats, Lee Trevino, is not much better. All of them, to a greater or lesser degree, take or took the club away from their body. All of them, equally, manage to get the club back on the line from ball to target early on in the downswing, and spot on by the hitting area.

A good backswing, alone, does not lead to a successful attack through the ball. The main reason is that your good backswing does not stop you hitting from the top on the downswing, or heaving around with your shoulders far too early. Superior golfers very seldom allow a clumsy shoulder movement into their swings but many have suffered spells when the hands get in too early, leading to the clubheads reaching the ball ahead of the hands, producing a steep, choppy action.

Obviously, the hands and arms should be relatively passive in the first part of the downswing. Many instructors have recognized this and produced their own formulas, of which the one-piece take-away, which undoubtedly helps take the hands out of the driving seat, is now universal amongst good players. Also popular is the deliberate thinking of making the hip turn the first movement in both backswing and downswing, but it produces one very drastic problem. If your body feeling going back is dominated by the hips alone, you will swing flat. If the same applies coming down, the shoulders will follow suit and the swing path will be across the ball. So, the hips are out. Even so, I believe we are remarkably close to finding the solution.

Take the club away from the ball with your movement centred on the upper thighs. This will include the hips, but what you feel should not be so

The backswing should feel like a coiling from the upper thighs.

that I can't recall any golfer worthy of the name with a poor leg action. Some people say the legs produce little of the power in a golf swing but all agree they are vital to a good swing path through the hitting area.

Look at golfers in your own club, even quite low handicappers. Notice how many have very poor leg movements, the whole of the swing dominated by the upper body, with no real base – the legs, that is – beneath it. Perhaps some of the world's top players have over-emphasized the role of the legs in the golf swing. They have argued, I think on occasion mistakenly, that they derive much of their power from this source. Against it, we have plenty of evidence that a Ballesteros can hit a drive over 200 yards when seated on a shooting stick or standing on one leg. Indeed, wind up your own body *without* using the arms and see what minimal acceleration you can achieve from legs and body alone. No, the legs are vital – but not for power.

One of the things on which Tony Jacklin worked the most at the peak of his career, urged on by Bert Yancey and Tom Weiskopf, was the importance of the legs. So also Jack Nicklaus, though he used to believe that legs are far more a power source than I do. He felt that he had relatively weak hands and knew that he had very strong legs, so assumed that power must derive from them.

If we think of the approach of two such mighty hitters as Nicklaus and Ballesteros when going for maximum length, there are interesting lessons to be learned. Both are emphatic that you take a bigger swing, getting the hands higher but that it must be *slow*. Thereafter they have entirely different key swing thoughts. Nicklaus is a believer in spinning the hips as fast as possible away from the ball, whereas Ballesteros thinks in terms of late and fast hand action. But the main point is both allow themselves time to let legs and hips lead the downswing.

much a turn as a coiling directly back and away from the ball. This is then followed by a turn of the body.

Being conscious of the legs from the start of the swing is enormously helpful when you reach the downswing stage and means that you ought to be able to begin this phase of the swing with the legs, not the hands and arms. Thereafter, let nature take its course. The rest will indeed be a reflex action.

While the importance of the legs in a good golf swing has commonly been stressed, they are not thought of in this respect. It's notable, however,

So, start away from the ball in one piece but with the legs leading and they should keep that lead for the remainder of the swing.

THE FOLLOW-THROUGH

As a TV commentator, I have exactly the same view of what's going on as you at home. You may even have the advantage of me. Perhaps you have a new TV set, there's nothing going on around you, and if the sun catches your screen you can always get up and draw the curtains. Our TV monitors have often seen many thousands of hours of use, technicians are moving around and we can't get up and draw the curtains. Instead, we have to rely on taping a few bits of cardboard around the monitor to try to shade it. I expect you sometimes get a little frustrated at home when one of us says, 'Not sure where that one went,'

when at home you can see it sailing straight down the middle.

However, even when I can't see, I can make an educated guess, based on the player's follow-through. I can often judge that he looks to have pulled, pushed, hooked or sliced his shot because of the position he reaches at the end of his swing. In many cases the follow-through is the result of what has gone before. The 'body talk' of the player is also helpful. For example, if he sways back on his heels, we can be fairly sure he can see his ball going to the right and doesn't like how far it is veering.

There are lessons you can learn from your own follow-through. If your leg action is rather stiff,

Two common poor follow-throughs – too early a turn of the shoulders *left* and too much effort *right*.

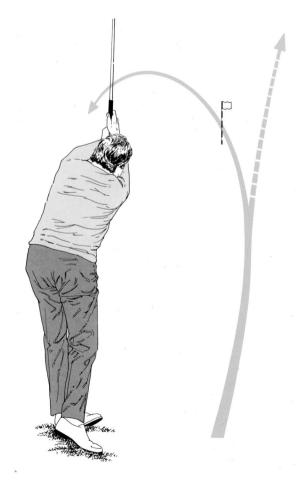

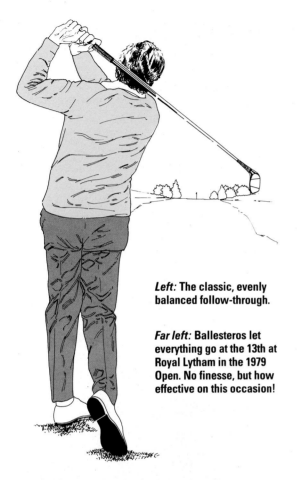

Left: The classic, evenly balanced follow-through.

Far left: Ballesteros let everything go at the 13th at Royal Lytham in the 1979 Open. No finesse, but how effective on this occasion!

HEAD MOVEMENT

Arnold Palmer, for one, believes that a still head was vital to his success. I seem also to remember Jack Nicklaus giving Tom Watson an impromptu lesson about head position and movement in practice before the Ryder Cup at Walton Heath in 1981.

There was a certain book, *A New Way to Better Golf* by Alex Morrison, which enjoyed quite a vogue when it was published in 1932. The author advocated that the golfer should keep his chin pointed behind the ball even until the completion of his swing. Chiropractors the length and breadth of the world blessed the name of Alex Morrison as the money poured in. No broken necks resulted but I'd wager a few ricked ones did!

In times past just about every professional believed and taught that the head must be still until the ball was struck. Nevertheless, let no one persuade you that it's possible to play golf without moving your head during the swing. Improvements in photography have proved beyond doubt that none of the players who *felt* they didn't move their heads were correct.

Many years ago I gave a lesson to a club golfer of good standard who was going through a bad patch. I could not work out why he was playing so dreadfully until suddenly it seemed to jump out a mile. When he reached the top of his very full backswing, his neck and shoulders had dragged his head round so far that neither of his eyes could see the ball. You may find this hard to believe but it was true. We worked on this for a while and there was some improvement. A few weeks later we both happened to be on the practice ground. I asked him how he was playing. 'Super', he replied, 'you were right. I really couldn't see the ball at the top.'

'Let's see you hit a few then,' I said gleefully.

He took out his driver and produced a steady flow of consistent shots. Mentally, I patted myself on the back for having produced the cure, and was just thinking that I should have charged him

perhaps even non-existent, you will never finish either in an elegant position or fully balanced. If your clubhead finishes low, this indicates that you have turned your shoulders much too early in the downswing, and have scythed at the ball, producing either a pull or slice, depending on the position of your clubface at impact.

The only exception to the evidence of a good or bad swing given by the follow-through is that if you hit with divine fire and fury, the momentum of your clubhead may 'knock' you off balance at the end – if your name is Seve Ballesteros, Gary Player or the young Arnold Palmer. Otherwise, use a bad finish to tell you something useful about how you swung at the ball.

double, when I looked at his head. He was turning it just as much as ever! Confidence plays such a vital role in golf.

Of course, this is an extreme example. You'd be unlikely to find yourself Open Champion one day with such a vast amount of head movement, especially with that little white ball disappearing from view at just the wrong moment. Yet many great players, such as Lee Trevino, Gary Player and Peter Thomson have a great deal of head movement. Research has been conducted into this by an American university. Thirty US professionals were studied, and it was found that on average at address, their heads were 3.1 inches behind the ball. By the top of the backswing, this had become 5.2 inches and increased to 6.1 at impact. That's just about 3 inches of lateral movement away from the ball from start to finish.

The same study found only a little less vertical movement. At the top of the swing, these thirty professionals had dipped 1.1 inches. At impact, the figure became 2.2 inches.

So, with all the weight of evidence that has built up in recent years, I cannot order you not to move you head. What I can do on the other hand, is look at the kinds of head movement that are not damaging to a good golf swing.

Let's take Jack Nicklaus as an example and see what happens to his head through his swing.

Just before he begins the backswing, Jack turns his head quite a bit to the right, so much so that I would estimate that he almost reaches a position where his nose comes between right eye and ball – but not quite. This is a very conscious movement on Jack's part. Basically, he gets most of the head movement out of the way early, before he really gets to work, surely a good thing. His head is not dragged out of position at the top of his backswing because Jack has already pre-set the position in the first movement.

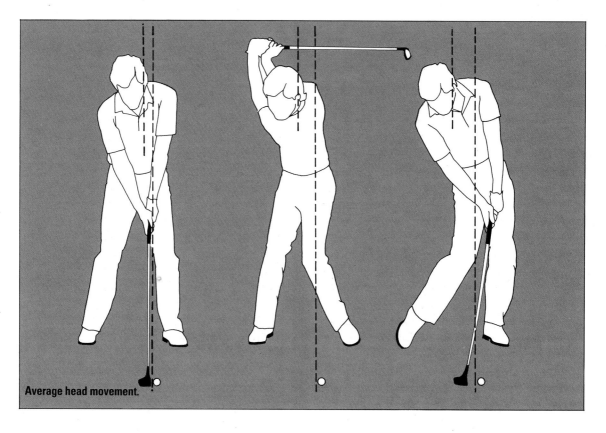

Average head movement.

Nicklaus's head movement
just before impact.

Thereafter the Nicklaus head remains remarkably quiet until he reaches the last few inches before impact. At this point, Jack lowers his head considerably, a little like a bull about to charge. At much the same time it begins to move laterally backwards. From a couple of feet before impact to the same distance into the follow-through the backward movement may be as much as 6 inches.

Gary Player makes an interesting comparison. In his case there is no pre-set turn but there is a slight one near the top of his backswing, caused by the pull of his very full shoulder turn on neck and head. As with Nicklaus, Gary lowers his head coming into the hitting area but there's little if any movement back from the ball.

And what of Arnold Palmer? Despite a swing much faster and more aggressive than the average, Palmer's head is the steadiest of my three examples. Unlike Nicklaus, he begins with his head turned a touch to the left. As with Player, there is a small but continuous turn that roughly follows the rhythm of his shoulder movement. There is no dip that I can discern in the hitting area and only a very slight lowering at and around impact. Palmer preaches the importance of the still head and he really does practise what he preaches, as far as I believe is humanly possible.

In my own case, I always felt that my head was steady. I'm very much a hands and arms player and had little, if any, lateral movement.

So what lessons should the good club player learn from these examples? Well, for a start you need some evidence. A video film is best. With it you can both see your swing in motion and also stop it frame by frame. Failing this, get a friend who's a competent photographer with a motor-

drive camera to take a series of shots of each stage of your swing. If you have not got access to a motor-drive camera, then take a series of photographs with a camera that has speeds at least up to 1/500th and do your swinging from exactly the same spot each time against a background that provides some points of reference – trees, fence posts or buildings. Your photographer must also remain in exactly the same place and take all his shots with the camera at the same height and angle.

When you are looking at the results, I hope you don't find any of the following faults:

1 Shoulders pull head around to excess.

2 Head sways laterally away from the ball on the backswing.

3 Head is lifted at the top of the swing by the shoulder turn.

4 Head moves laterally *forward* in the hitting area or earlier.

Above: There should be little head movement throughout the swing.

Right: Four common faults.

Perhaps the last of these is the most serious. My number 3 is not much better. It means that you are lifting the club to the top of the swing rather than your backswing being a smooth, windmill-like turning movement. If your head is moving forward as you come into the ball, this means in essence that you are throwing your body into the shot. Try always to have the feeling that you are hitting the ball *away* from you, not heaving into it with shoulders, stomach or indeed with any part of your anatomy except hands and arms, and that your legs are gliding smoothly along the target path.

If you find faults, they can be very hard to remove from an ingrained golf swing. Have a friend place his hand on the top of your head as you make both practice and swings in earnest. This will prove a most effective check and reveal what progress you are making.

However, I hope we've seen that some head movement is inevitable unless you are exceptionally flexible at the base of your neck. This being so, it's not practicable to try to feel your swing as a turning movement around your head as a fixed point. Better instead, if this is one of

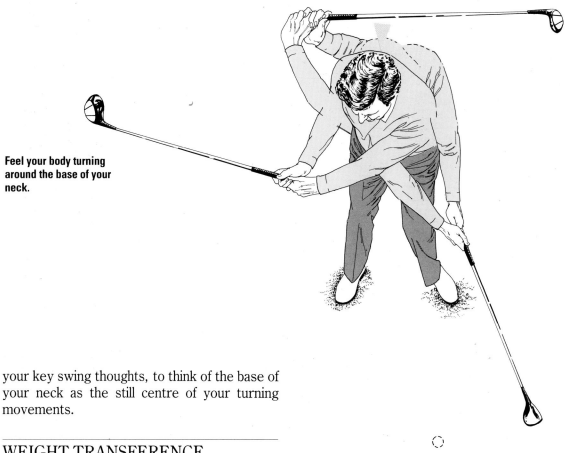

Feel your body turning around the base of your neck.

your key swing thoughts, to think of the base of your neck as the still centre of your turning movements.

WEIGHT TRANSFERENCE

This is undoubtedly one of the great mysteries of golf. It's also essential to playing your best golf in terms of achieving your own maximum distance.

Many golfers don't really transfer their weight at all. At address, they stand with their weight roughly shared fifty-fifty between either foot. During the backswing it does not move to the rear. It can remain fairly constant or even move more strongly on to the front foot. This is caused, more than anything else, by the player lifting the club up, ready for a chop down, not a sweep. Then, the higher the clubhead goes, the more the weight goes on to the front foot.

With this kind of swing, there is no prospect whatsoever of your hitting a long ball. I am reminded of James Braid, the British Open Cham-

pion five times early this century who, it was once said, drove 'with divine fury'. Certainly he was much the longest from the tee of the Great Triumvirate of J. H. Taylor, Harry Vardon and Braid himself.

Yet James Braid was not 'born' a long hitter. It's claimed he merely arrived at a golf course one day and, lo and behold, had become one overnight. Why? How? Obviously there couldn't have been a sudden increase in strength. Equally, as Braid was already a very good golfer indeed, it's hardly likely that his timing could have improved enough in such a short period of time to make so dramatic a difference.

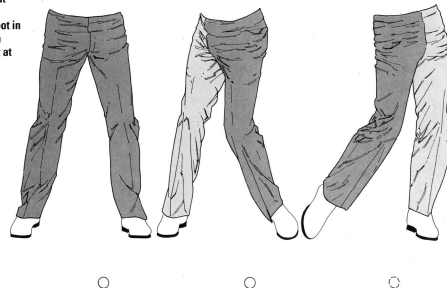

The weight is equally distributed on your feet at the address, but moves slightly on to the back foot in the backswing, and then flows on to the front foot at impact.

No, in my opinion, Braid must have suddenly achieved the knack of 'punching his weight' or transferring his weight from back foot to front foot. Before, I imagine, he must have been solely a hands and arms player.

I think we can see weight transference happening most clearly in the swings of several great players who have what is usually considered a fairly serious fault in a golf swing – lateral sway. Walter Hagen, the Irishmen Fred Daly and Joe Carr, Peter Thomson, Lee Trevino and Tom Weiskopf all sway from the ball and again into it on the downswing – a movement of beauty when they do it. Quite obviously, their body weight must go to and fro also. In contrast, Tom Watson and Jack Nicklaus don't appear to sway. Their swings, as indeed is my own, are far more an up and down movement.

Yet we are all long hitters. We too transfer the weight into the ball but without real lateral movement. As far as I know, in each case this happened perfectly naturally, but I have advice for those less fortunate.

Most golfers will have at least slightly more weight on their back foot when they have taken up their stance. This is as a result of the rear shoulder being set a deal lower than the leading one.

However, on the backswing far more weight must be transferred. This will happen if you get your front knee bending in towards the ball, perhaps even behind it. This ensures that the weight moves off the front foot because it's just about impossible to make that knee movement with much weight on the front foot. If you try, you'll fall over!

So far, so good but, of course, your weight may *remain* on the backfoot so you are only using your hands and arms in hitting, and therefore lose power. The secret is to begin your downswing with active legs and hips and feel the front knee getting back to the ball with the clubhead.

Anyone who 'hits from the top', with hands, arms and shoulders alone, will never manage to transfer weight effectively. What power he or she gets will come almost entirely from the hands and arms.

AT FULL
POWER

A useful way of dividing golf into its various components is in
terms of how much clubhead speed is involved. Sometimes, we
need to hit very nearly full out, at others we are thinking far more
of control but still using a more or less full swing but at a slower
pace, and thirdly there are shots where we are striking the ball
quite gently, as in chipping and putting. The power shots are the
ones that give most players most pleasure, because of the
satisfaction of taking a good swing and watching the ball fly, but in
reality the essence of good driving is in achieving the optimum
distance, not necessarily the maximum distance, without losing
direction and control.

There is no time in golf when we should allow ourselves to hit totally full out, with no thought given to control. However, I'd be the last to deny that, for some players, much of the appeal of golf lies in hitting a ball as far as possible with the driver

Every year, before the American PGA Championship, a long driving competition is held. Each contestant is allowed three attempts and at least one drive must finish on the fairway. In due course, a 'long-driving champion' emerges.

But to be quite frank, I would not rate some of the contestants as 'golfers'. They can sometimes be little more than gorillas, looking as if they have been kept caged up to be allowed out for their one moment of the year. Their handicaps are often high, although there are also some powerful young pros with very good swings.

It is quite possible to hit a golf ball a very long way while being off balance and with appalling leg action – to name just two of the faults on view.

However, these ferocious gentlemen must be doing something right and indeed they are. For maximum distance there are six basic rules:

1 The highest possible controllable clubhead speed must be attained.

2 The clubhead must be square to the target.

3 The clubhead must be travelling parallel with the ground or just slightly on the rise.

4 The clubhead must be travelling on the line of ball and target, that is, without either an in-to-out or out-to-in swing path.

5 The sweet spot of the clubhead must meet the ball flush in the middle of the back.

6 The angle of attack must be correct.

Some of these essentials apply to any golf shot where the aim is to hit straight but not, of course,

Tom Watson exemplifies the simplicity of a good swing allied to a feeling of power. Aim for a wide backswing arc.

Watson is a good example
of getting the hands high at
the top of the backswing.

'highest possible clubhead speed'. Most of what I have to say concerns how to develop this.

Going for distance

To start, I want to illustrate from my own experience. Although I was a long driver throughout my tournament career of about twenty years, I did have phases during which I might have been scoring well and driving safely but my length was drastically reduced. I remember a phase during the 1963 season when I was not able to move the ball much more than 220 yards. Looking back on it, I had then some of the faults of a handicap golfer. On the backswing, I broke my wrists far too early (not a fault for everyone), took the club back on an outside line and then lifted it to the top,

which I reached without making either my usual full turn of shoulder or right hip. Everything was curtailed, in fact with the clubhead pointing left of target. Coming back to the ball, I was hurried, chopped down and was pulling my arms in towards my body at impact. I also stayed back on my right side and my left hip cleared too early. It all meant I was operating at 70 per cent power.

Already, I think any competent golfer will be able to see some of the don'ts, which will probably have cropped up from time to time in his or her own game.

What, however, was happening in my own swing when I was driving at my maximum length? Looking back, it now seems to me that the most important single factor was that I had plenty of

The movement back towards the ball starts with the upper legs and hips.

time, especially in the backswing. I moved the clubhead away from the ball smoothly and without hurry. Nothing was rushed in that take and turn-away from the ball all the way to the horizontal. There was all the time in the world to complete the turn of hips and shoulders. At the top, I did not consciously pause, as has often been recommended. Instead, I began the downswing in a fairly leisurely way but with the feeling that I was building up to a total freewheeling release of right arm and hand into and through the back of the ball and through to the target.

Well, you may be saying, that's easier said than done, and there have certainly been times in my own career when I should have agreed with you whole-heartedly. So far, I've been talking about less than a handful of key points and about the feel of both a bad and a good long-driving swing. It is time to go into the details of what make for long driving, or gaining your own maximum length.

First, aim at the widest arc possible in the backswing because this stretches all your golfing muscles. Start back keeping the club relatively low to the ground and avoid swinging quickly inside. I was an early breaker of the wrists, as is Johnny Miller amongst a few others, but I am inclined to agree with Jack Nicklaus who feels that delaying this movement to the end of the backswing does help to ensure a full shoulder turn. Continue swinging back relatively slowly. Many swing back more quickly when they are attempting a big hit. The shoulder turn and body wind-up must be as full as possible. You should also make a determined effort to get your hands high, 'reaching for the sky' Nicklaus calls it (Tom Watson, if anything, gets his hands even higher than Jack). The full turn plus the high hands mean that you've got your clubhead the maximum distance away from the ball. You've given yourself room to develop pace back to the ball.

At this point, however, note that I've said nothing about length of backswing. Once the club goes past the horizontal, it's highly likely that the cause is simply that you have allowed the clubhead to drop. As a result, you really have to lift it up with the hands as you begin the downswing. Nothing has been gained in power by letting the clubhead fall beyond the horizontal. Just get it there, or just short. Players of the past used to raise the club

above the horizontal and there are a few examples today, notably the 1984 US Masters champion, Ben Crenshaw. In fact, his is a case that helps prove my point, for his excessively long backswing could well be the reason why Ben, throughout his career, has hit more wild shots than many other top players. He still has what we call an 'amateur swing'. Others look more taut and controlled and many find that a three-quarter backswing gives them enough distance from the ball to develop both full power and control.

Having completed the backswing, the most important part of the job is done. At least in theory, the downswing should follow as a reflex action. It is more likely to, if the backswing has

Left: **You reach maximum speed in the downswing before impact. (The sequence starts with the gray plane.)**

been right. However, when trying to produce an extra long drive, a player may try to lash from the top with hands and arms. These must not be the first to move in the downswing. That privilege belongs to the lower body. You must have the feeling that the leading leg and hip begin the movement back towards the ball, the hands coming late. Hitting early really means starting to lash with hands and arms from the top. Hitting late, though, is a dangerous image to have in your golfing mind's eye. It is a folly to try to feel that you are reaching maximum speed at impact. No good player does it. Instead, he or she actually reaches maximum speed before impact and more or less maintains the pace of his or her swing through the hitting area. In fact, several scientific studies have shown that the clubhead has actually slowed a little by the time it reaches ball, although no one, good or bad, ever feels that they are actually decelerating as they reach the ball, except when foozling a little chip or when putting. Finally, for that big hit, try experimenting with your stance, putting your feet either further apart or closer together. A wide stance tends to cut down on the hand and arm action; the narrow one makes the hip turn more full. One of these opposites will be best suited to your swing.

Below: **A wide stance tends to restrict the hand movement *left,* while a narrow one produces a greater whip in the swing.**

THE SAFE DRIVE

Many people, even quite knowledgeable golfers, seem to think the greatest players are those who hit the ball the furthest and straightest.

This just isn't true. Most of the greatest players have only been 'long enough'. By this I mean that without a wind in their face they are able to get up in two comfortably at the long par 4s and par 5s which aren't over 510 yards. My great contemporaries Bobby Locke and Peter Thomson were two such players. Part of their golfing philosophy was that the first essential was to get the ball on the fairway. The real game of golf began after that.

Because they were so consistent, I believe they could have lived comfortably enough with the more powerful players who have succeeded them in international golf.

Bobby Locke, many years ago, told me a story which concerned the leading American amateur of his day, Frank Stranahan, a fellow who used to travel around the world with full weight-lifting kit at the ready. Not surprisingly, he was long from the tee.

Said Stranahan to Locke: 'You know, Bobby, you are too short off the tee.'

Replied Locke: 'You'd better read Saturday morning's papers, Frank.'

This was at the Troon Open Championship of 1950. At the time, Locke held a lead of some half-dozen strokes over Stranahan, and when the event finished, as was usual in those days, late on Friday afternoon, Locke was champion, with the American many strokes behind in 9th place – although he did set the amateur championship record, which still stands, with a 66 in the last round.

Locke's point was that, yes, Stranahan was outdriving him time and again by many yards. All too often, however, the final few yards took the ball into deep heather, a bunker or other hazard. Meanwhile, Locke was sedately making his way to mid-fairway.

Even so, Locke was hurt. Somewhere inside him, perhaps, there was a savage hitter longing to get out!

The point here about safe driving is that the shorter you hit, the less likely you are to finish in trouble. At least geometry is on your side. The shot off-line by, say, 15 degrees may not reach the rough. A longer drive will.

How many golfers, I wonder, of even quite low handicaps would score better on average if they contented themselves with an iron from the tee all the way round. There'd be few birdies but equally few double bogeys.

But can I detect a cry of protest? 'What?' you are saying. 'Does this fellow Alliss want us to burn all our woods and lose all the joy of the golf ball soaring high, long and handsome?' Even if I did, I know I'd be attempting the impossible. So on to stage two of my argument, the whole of which is really about keeping the ball on the fairway – the safe drive of my heading.

On then, too, to the second myth. Most followers of golf have heard that Jack Nicklaus likes to play with a little fade on his shots, and that Ben Hogan only became a consistent winner of major championships when he rid himself of his long, low, hooking flight and cultivated a Nicklaus-like fade. Nevertheless, they've seen the young assistant pro or low handicap men drawing the ball and they want to do the same or, better still, send it away to fairway or flag like a ruled line.

Neither shape of shot is in fact ideal for safe driving. A consistent fade is much better all along the line.

Just as it is impossible consistently to hit the ball straight, it is equally impossible to be nearly as consistent at drawing the ball as fading it. Just think of some medium handicappers at your own club. The man who fades every shot, as long as he makes a balanced swing through the ball, never seems to produce a wild slice. Another man who draws the ball, of about the same standard of general play, seems to have really quite dreadful days. Suddenly, none of his drives seem to start off where aimed in order to drift back to the middle of the fairway. There's a succession of low hooks

Given that you will not
necessarily hit the ball
exactly where you want to,
a short drive is often safer
than a long one.

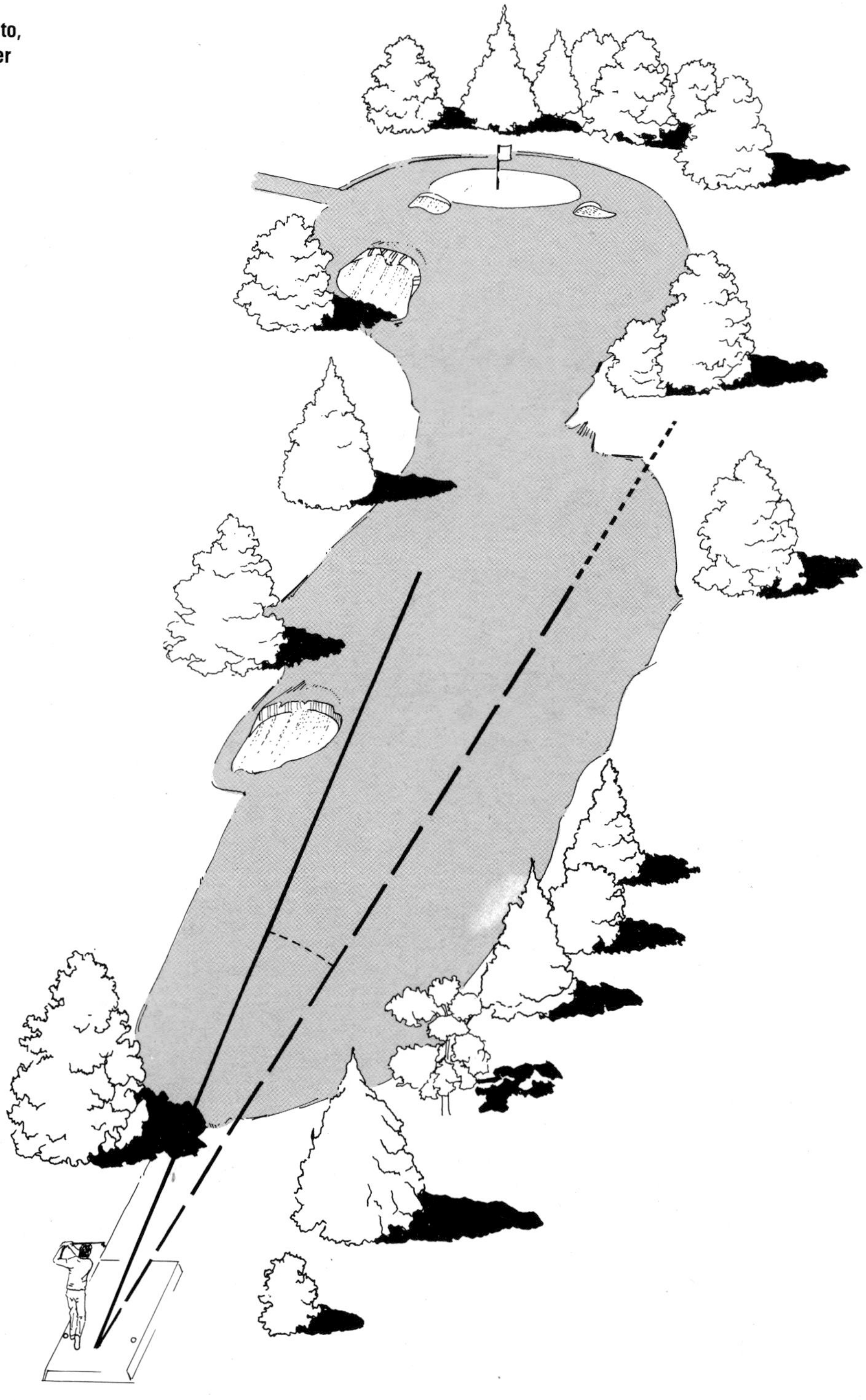

that turn through the air very sharply indeed and run into trouble. As if this isn't disaster enough, he also gets into trouble on the other side of the fairway when his draw doesn't 'take'.

The reason is the one I started off with. It's more 'natural' to fade. So, if you're a right hander, aim it down the left side of the fairway. Some will stay there, the rest curl across to the middle. Even on your off days your troubles will be fewer. Ask Trevino, he knows.

FAIRWAY WOODS

For many long-hitting professionals, these clubs are more often used for a safe tee shot than from the fairway itself. I want first to follow their example and stress how much better good club golfers (and not so good!) would score if they made far more use of their 3 or 4 woods for tee shots and perhaps settled overall for driving with a club of the loft, say, of a 2 wood.

As it's more natural to fade, allow for this in aiming your drive down the fairway.

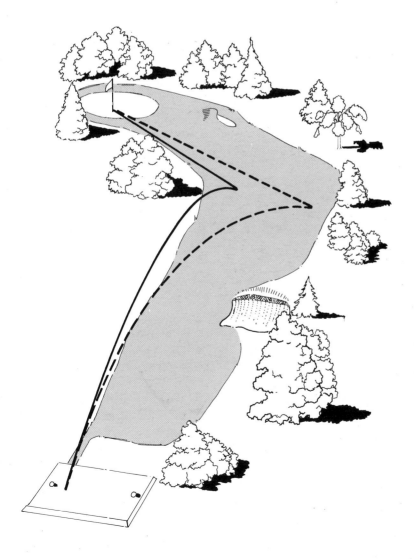

The slightly shorter shaft must make it more easy to control the clubhead throughout the swing. What this means, in effect, is that you will actually be a longer hitter with a 3 wood than you will using a long-shafted, deep-faced, straight-faced driver. I do not mean by this that a great swing and hit with a 3 wood will send the ball further than a driver. I'm talking about *average* length, which takes straightness into account.

Try this experiment. Go out one day without your driver and tot up the distances you achieve from hole to hole with your 3 wood, eventually arriving at your grand total for the average of perhaps fourteen holes. Next time, use your driver throughout. I'll wager that your *total* yardage will be better for day 1 than day 2.

Mainly, this will be because you've hit fewer *destructive* shots. Because of its length of shaft and lack of loft, the driver is the most difficult club in the bag. Even the greatest players very seldom manage a round where they hit every shot in the middle of the club and hold the fairway as well. Take Tom Watson, for instance, one of the most consistent challengers for major championship honours in golf. As television is perhaps best at showing shots on and around the green, it must seem that Tom seldom makes a serious error. Not so. He is one of the best drivers in modern golf but nevertheless does miss a lot of fairways when not on peak form. So Watson, like Nicklaus before him and his contemporary Severiano Ballesteros, normally only uses his driver when he needs the extra length – on par 5s, long 4s or perhaps when he thinks he can get up with his tee shot at a short 4.

If you put severe hook or slice spin on the ball with a driver, the resulting swerve through the air will be abrupt and uncontrollable. With a 3 wood it will be far more gentle. Indeed, the actual result may well be quite a nice position to left or right of the fairway rather than deep into dense rough.

Consider, also, that very often the extra length you may get from a good drive may be of very little practical use. Ask yourself if you are actually better at playing a gentle pitch with a controlled swing rather than a firmer shot from further away, which will give you more backspin.

Finally, I'd ask you to note that position to left or right of the fairway is usually far more important than sheer distance down it. How often we noticed at the 1984 Open Championship at St Andrews that the 'safe' line which tended to avoid serious trouble was also the worst direction from which to play the shot to the green. Right-handed hookers will miss most of the bunkering and out of bounds, but the ideal line from the tee is always as close as you dare to danger down the right-hand side. Think of the 18th. If you are almost out of bounds down the right in front of Rusacks Hotel, the Valley of Sin is not in play. You can putt onto the green!

Don't just reach for your driver. Think first about what you're trying to achieve with your tee shot. It ought to be that you want to get to the best position for playing your next to the green. So, often a fairway wood will be the club to use. Banish from your minds that nonsensical expression: 'You drive for show'. A good driver who can hold his own on the greens is a match for anyone, as Langer and Calvin Peete have proved.

Of course, many golfers think of fairway woods as the clubs they hit for long shots from the fairway and that alone. If you feel that you are rather inconsistent with these clubs, I suggest you consider your basic technique and mental attitude.

Whisking the ball away

As a tournament player, I was always entirely happy at the prospect of whisking the ball away from a hard glassy lie or the opposite, soft and even muddy conditions underfoot. This kind of sweeping stroke without benefit of a tee peg, does, however, need a very exact path into the ball. I was helped by the fact that I never took deep divots. I played with the mental picture of the clubhead clipping the ball away.

However, disaster is so much nearer when your ball is cushioned by dense fairway grass.

You may wish to consider whether or not you

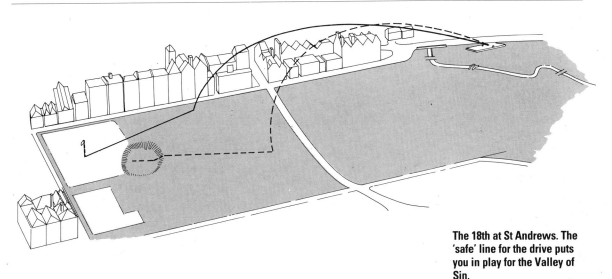

The 18th at St Andrews. The 'safe' line for the drive puts you in play for the Valley of Sin.

would achieve better results by coming into the ball on a more downward path, making very much the same swing at the ball as you would with a long iron and always taking a divot. So many good iron players at club level may also be good drivers, but poor players of the fairway woods. I suspect that they are confident when hitting down and through with irons, and parallel or even up from a tee peg. For them, the fairway wood is very much an in-between shot and they lack confidence. Make sure you have clubs that help you. Try out both deep and shallow-faced clubs, large and small heads. A club with the shaft length of a 4 iron with plenty of loft and extra lead may well help you. It's why the baffy used to be popular long ago. Experimentation can be well worth the time and effort. Basically, it is only possible to whisk the ball away from unfavourable lies with a fairway wood if you are an exceedingly exact striker. So put yourself to the test. Go out on your club's practice ground, take out your 3 or 4 wood and *don't* nudge your ball into an inviting lie much the same as if it were on a tee peg. Instead, try hitting from rather bare lies, or with the ball in a slight hollow or wet patch – lies, in fact, that you would not fancy any too strongly out on the golf course. It is possible to half plug a ball, hit the top half and it'll spin its way out, providing the swing is a sweeping, not chopping one.

If you are successful, you have the ability to whisk them away clean. Otherwise, try hitting down just slightly at the ball. This allows just that fraction of an inch more margin for error, because the steeper attack on the ball may well keep you

Sweeping the ball away from a carpet-pile fairway.

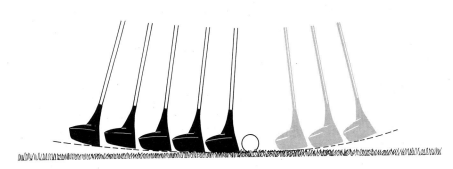

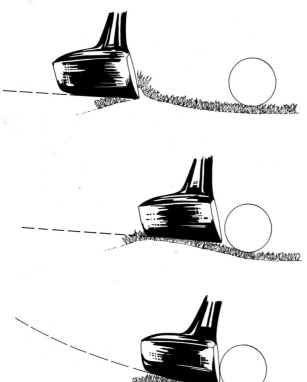

A downward hit allows for any undulations behind the ball.

sensible course will usually be to reach for nothing less lofted than a 9 iron (a sand wedge may well be the safest club to use) and be content to sacrifice a stroke but get the ball back on the fairway.

However, if the lie is none too frightening, your fairway woods should be much more effective than a 4 or 5 iron. Woods push through the grass, rather than cutting through as an iron does. This means that there is far more chance of preventing the clubhead twisting. A club with a small head is better and something between a 4 and a 7 wood can be ideal.

Woods push through long grass where irons get entangled.

just clear of, say, the very slight undulation which prevents you getting at the back of the ball when you have that sweeping flat clubhead path. It may also be closer to your personal technique with the irons.

FROM THE ROUGH

I'm sure many a club golfer has noticed a sad shake of the head from his partner when he's taken a fairway wood from the rough – and failed miserably. His partner is one of those who thinks it's very rash and greedy to use a wood once you're off the fairway. Well of course it may be. If the ball is lying very well down, or there's a clump of grass or heather between you and the ball, the most

DOING AWAY WITH THE LONG IRONS

Confidence is at least half of golf. If you have little trust in your ability to hit anything above a 5 iron, why carry on through the years with the millstone round your neck of having to use the high irons? Probably a 6 wood will best fit the bill. Its short shaft makes it easier to control than less lofted fairway woods. You'll find, too, that because you'll soon be using it a lot you will learn from experience how to vary your shots. It is a versatile club which, on the one hand, can give you considerable length, while you can also choke down the grip and swing more gently when less is needed. It's no disgrace not to be able to hit a 3 iron some 190 yards. What counts is the results you get from your clubs.

How things have changed! This old driver, from Nairn Golf Club, is over a hundred years old. Compare its shape with that produced by today's technology.

BUYING FAIRWAY WOODS

For many years now, manufacturers have preached the advantages of 'the matched set'. Sidle up to a few tournament players on the practice ground and have a look at their clubs. The name of some well-known club maker may be emblazoned upon the huge bag but the clubs inside may be of very great variety. Most of the time, the one or two fairway woods each player carries will be tried and trusted friends. Jack Nicklaus, for instance, kept the same 3 wood for many years. For me, the old way of going into the pro's shop and looking around was far more fun than buying a matched set and, just every once in a while, led to finding a club much treasured for years. It was done by feel. Nevertheless, the 'matched set' was, and is, excellent sales promotion – far better to sell clubs by the dozen than singly! It can also be a good idea to experiment with a 'driving iron'. Many tournament players carry a Ping 1 iron with quite a light head and

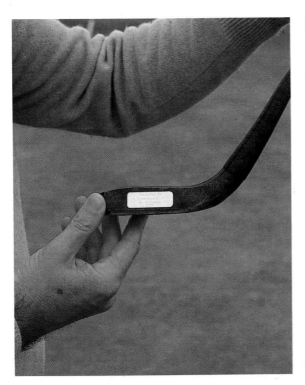

longer shaft. They can hit it 230 yards, straight, and need carry just two woods in their sets.

Don't be totally seduced by that glittering set of clubs on the stand. All that glistens is not gold. Once you have found a club in which you have got confidence, keep faithful to it. It will naturally receive fairly rough treatment from frequent contact with the turf and the odd stone (or someone steps on it) but you can always have it refurbished by your professional. Make a friend of him. Of course, you'll have to pay for craftsmanship but you'll get more free advice from him than a lawyer!

When you are actually trying to find clubs that suit you, there is no substitute for trial and error. But in the first place, the club must look right to you when you set it behind the ball, and feel right when you swing it. Some players come to favour small-headed clubs with quite deep faces while others prefer a bigger head with a shallow face. This may depend on where you normally play golf. If there are often tight lies, and certainly on links courses the shallow face is likely to be best. The deep-face clubs are more suited to well-cushioned lies as it can be more difficult to get the ball airborne from them.

VARYING THE FLIGHT

When you need maximum distance, lessen the loft on the clubface. This will give a lower flight, less backspin and, of course, more run on the ball.

Unlike many golfers, I can remember hardly a single shot from my entire career. However, there's one particular one that sticks firmly in my mind, and it's of the kind I was just describing.

It came in the 1965 Ryder Cup matches at Royal Birkdale. In the morning fourballs Arnold Palmer and Dave Marr – then PGA champion and now a fellow commentator with ABC in America – had beaten Christy O'Connor and me with some ease by 6 and 5. We weren't pleased as we had a good Ryder Cup record together. We drew the same pair again in the afternoon and this time fared better. It was a tremendous battle but we came to the last hole, then still a par 5, one up. Of course, we needed a birdie to be virtually sure things at least stayed that way. The green was almost out of reach so an eagle was highly unlikely.

I had hit the longest drive and watched as the others played their second shots. Marr got his to within some forty yards of the green. O'Connor, bunkered with his tee shot, recovered some ninety yards down the fairway. Palmer then sent his into a greenside bunker on the right.

If I could get up now, it would almost certainly clinch the match. I was carrying just two woods, a driver and a 4. I seldom felt confident with this particular driver from the fairway, so the 4 wood it had to be. Yet I didn't really think it was enough club. It looked an awfully long way to that green surrounded by masses of people.

I toed the clubhead in just a touch (a tip I'd got from John Jacobs) and told myself to keep the hands ahead at impact – and let rip. It flew right out of the button towards the right front of the green with about 5 or 6 yards of draw. It pitched some thirty yards short, gave one good bounce and stopped just fifteen feet short of the hole. That birdie was now a formality.

In the end, I wasn't even asked to putt. Dave Marr flicked my ball up, thus conceding both the hole and the match. I knew I'd never hit a finer fairway wood in my life. The lower flight and slight draw had given me perhaps an extra thirty yards – and a win.

This kind of shot also gives an ideal flight for playing into wind. However well you may strike the ball, the last thing you want is height. For an even lower flight, which I didn't need on that occasion, move the ball back a couple of inches or so in your stance. Concentrate on making a good hit. Swing well within yourself to make this more likely.

The ball will tend to fly lower if you grip down the shaft and higher if you hold the club right at the end. Of course, you'll get a little less power from the shorter club but the low flight will compensate for that. Use a three-quarter swing and a slower tempo. Pace, direction and angle of attack eighteen inches either side of the ball are all-important. It can also help to get low flight if you play this shot with fairly 'dead' wrists and try to have the feeling of pulling through the ball.

Use the same techniques if you're trying to keep the ball low under an obstacle, say, an overhanging branch. Don't use a club with too little loft as your ball may never get properly off the ground. If you have an iron to the green, use a 4 or 5, not, say, your 2.

The 18th at Royal Birkdale in the 1965 Ryder Cup. Toeing in the 4 wood gave me enough distance to reach the green in two.

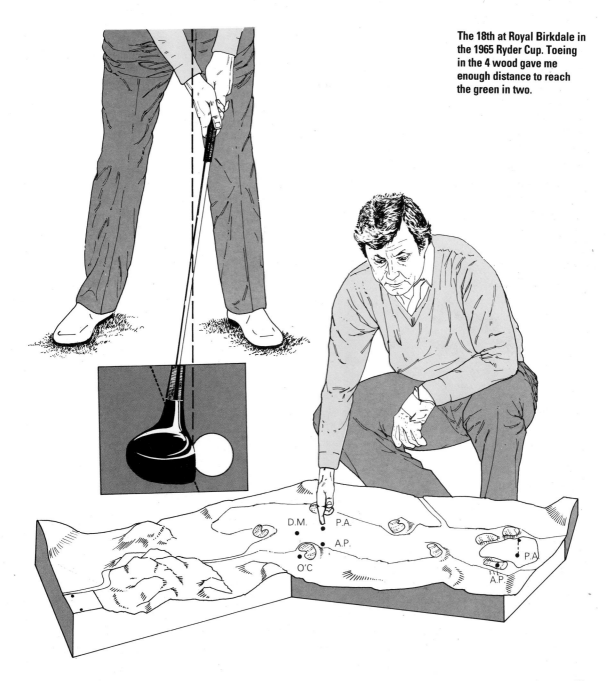

High flight can be equally useful, perhaps vital, with fairway woods (or any club in the bag) in various situations. These are the most common:

1 If there's a strong following wind, it will carry a 3 or 4 wood played from a medium height tee peg much further than a lower driver shot. The wind will also take some of the backspin off the ball so in average fairway conditions you'll still get a reasonable amount of run. Don't try anything tricky, and don't change either your stance or ball position. Let the loft of the clubhead do its work, using your normal swing, without hitting harder.

2 A fairway wood shot will usually not hold the green when the flight is low, not, that is, unless the green is very receptive. You will have far more chance of success if your ball comes plummeting down. With this in mind, play the ball a little forward in your stance, open the stance a touch, aim away from the flag, allowing for fade, and hope your ball pitches, slows and drifts along towards the flag. It's a shot that gives me enormous satisfaction.

3 On many parkland courses one is often blocked out for the second shot by stands of trees. It is easy enough to knock an 8 iron over the top, perhaps, but you'd finish well short of the green. You need both height and length. Do very much the same as I advise above, but be a little more extreme and add one more ingredient: be wristy and slide the clubhead under the ball. It's amazing how quickly a 4 wood will soar upwards.

PLAYING WITH FADE

Most club golfers aim to hit with draw, but, in fact, the fade is a far better thing to aim for. Many top players have worked at giving themselves the fade shot as it is the safest in golf.

These photographs of the address and top of the backswing show the different stances and swings for hitting straight *left*, hitting with fade *centre*, and hitting with draw *right*. Open the stance and play the ball further forward for fade; shut the stance and play the ball further back for draw.

Most of these professionals did probably begin their golfing development with a draw, and may still have a swing shape that would bring about the occasional hook unless they made adjustments. The most usual such adjustment is to make ball contact with a very slightly open face, which is, however, moving along the target line. Basically, this approach is at the centre of Jack Nicklaus's technique, and except on certain courses, of which Augusta in the Masters is certainly one, he always tries to play with a fade.

This is how I fade the ball. I open my stance, play the ball further forward and weaken my left hand grip so that just one knuckle shows. I have my hands ahead of the clubhead, break my wrists early and maintain that wrist position through the ball. For draw, I do exactly the reverse, using one club less loft.

Ben Hogan, on the other hand, a violent hooker in his early days before he became a winner, had a slightly different approach. He 'weakened' his left-hand grip until his left thumb went directly

Moving the hands down the grip, keeping the hands ahead and having the ball a couple of inches further back produces a lower flight.

Ben Hogan

down the top of the shaft, perhaps even a little to the left. This, he always felt, made more or less sure that he never came into the ball with the clubface shut.

Lee Trevino is the outstanding propagandist of the fade. He considers it absolutely essential for golf at the highest level. Yet, like Ben Hogan, he is a natural hooker and has the clubhead in an extremely shut position at the top of the back-swing, normally a recipe for hooking disasters. Trevino only avoids hooking because of various antidotes he has built into his swing. For instance, he stands more wide open than any other good

player I have ever seen. Indeed, I doubt if I've seen even a club 'hacker' with a truly horrendous slice stand more open than Lee. But this alone wouldn't be enough to stop the hook, although it undoubtedly helps him to cut across the line of flight from out to in. He combines it with very pronouced leg drive, which enables him to get his clubface square to the ball at impact.

These players know their own swings very well indeed. Just as important, when in form, they can both vary their swings and put little adjust-ments into effect. Certainly, if they hit a banana slice unintentionally, they will know the cause.

THE IRONS

If wooden-club play can at least sometimes be concerned with sheer length, that is just never the name of the game with irons. Here, it doesn't matter what the number on the club, or how far you hit with it, but how near you can get the ball to the target. Usually, you are playing to a green or the flag itself. However, at long last club golfers are beginning to learn from the professionals they watch at tournaments or on television and are using irons to play from a tee peg to the fairway, in order, perhaps, to avoid trouble, but also to set themselves up in the ideal place from which to play the rest of the hole. The target remains: not the green or flag now, but the ideal place on the fairway. This is the point of iron play, getting to the best position.

THE LONG IRONS

The 1, 2 and 3 irons are the clubs that sort out the men from the boys (not a few quite good club golfers find the 4 none too easy either!).

A piece of research was done at a Dunlop Masters tournament during the 1960s into what areas of play left most scope for improvement. Amongst the players selected through the green, there was a very clear answer indeed – you've guessed – the long irons. In real terms the success rate at hitting greens was much less impressive than, say, the players' expertise at getting the short irons close to the hole, driving on to fairways, bunker play and short putting.

While you can severely limit your use of these clubs and substitute a couple of lofted woods if

things become intolerable, if you're really basically a better iron- than wooden-club player, there is extra incentive to mastering the long irons as you will lack confidence in woods, whatever the degree of loft.

Why do so many players find long irons the most difficult clubs in the bag, not excluding the driver? How should you face and overcome the difficulties?

We are back again with the length of shaft and lack of loft. Most good golfers would experience little difficulty in handling a 2 iron competently, despite the lack of loft, if the head were attached to a shaft of, say, 8 iron length. The lower the number on an iron head, the further the ball is away from the body, and that does make handling more of a problem.

Clubheads also pose a psychological problem for many golfers. Undeniably, the long irons often look both small and thin, lacking the encouraging bulk of the short irons. Often, too, these clubs can feel too light. Even the low-handicap club golfer 'doesn't know quite where the head is' during his swing. If that's so, there is little chance of playing a reasonable stroke.

My own irons, which I've been faithful to for some dozen years, are very heavy and I do believe that helps most of us. For some thirty years, I've used a swing weight of E8, which those of you with knowledge of this topic will immediately realize is exceptionally heavy. I have thick grips and extra stiff shafts. These heavy clubs best suit my rhythm, and I fear the featherlight clubs which began to enjoy great popularity in 1984 wouldn't

The different lengths of an iron and a driver.

Jack Nicklaus in the perfect position. The hands, head and knees are all absolutely right.

suit me at all. Yet, in idle moments I've picked up the long irons of Nicklaus and Weiskopf and been amazed at how light they are, and how they feel just like swinging a stick. I really don't know how these maestros can 'feel' the clubhead throughout their swings.

One way to approach the difficulty of handling long irons is simply to limit the number you use. If you have a set of irons that you're well satisfied with, let's say the 4 to wedge, then you could reserve your 2 or 3 irons mostly for high days and holidays. After all, it's a waste of time, expendi-

ture and energy to carry a long iron you do not really want to use; say, for a shot where you know you need a 3 you play your 4 because you have more confidence in the club, even though you know you will be short.

Another solution is purely practice. I know of no substitute for the thrill of cracking a really good long iron away. Anyone can catch a driver shot in the middle now and again, but there are golfers by the thousand who've never experienced a really good hit with a long iron.

If you're willing to devote the time and have

some aptitude, I can promise that you will get the feel of your long irons. Alas, the prolonged practice session over, that feel may soon go – on the instant if you hit a couple of stinging thin ones out on the course the very next day. The long irons are surely the most difficult clubs.

If your long irons feel light in the hands, far more so than your short and mid-irons, it is worth resorting to a roll of lead tape. There is nothing *infra dig* about this – a lot of tournament players use it. Your local professional will almost certainly have a roll and you can do a bit of the experimenta-

A full set of irons.

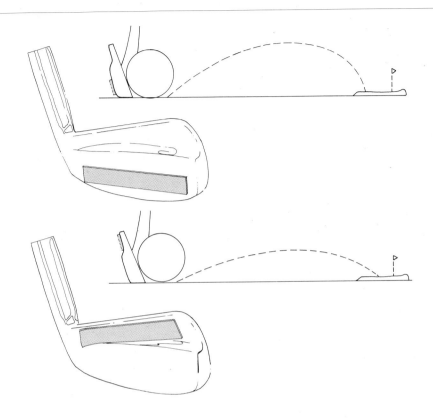

Weighted tape on the bottom of an iron gives more height, on the top less height.

tion that, to me, is always part of the fun of golf.

Place these sticky strips on the back of the club selected for the treatment, parallel with either the bottom or top edges, trying different positions until you like the feel of the club. It won't take much to make quite a dramatic difference. Placing the tape to the bottom will tend to give you more height on your shots and to the top less height. If you are normally a fairly straight hitter, but fade or even slice the long irons, try some tape towards the toe. It may be the answer.

However, most clubs are scientifically designed in the first place and this rather rough-and-ready method may unbalance them. If you get it wrong no permanent harm is done – just peel the tape off again.

How hard you hit with the long irons is also very important. Some players find that hitting in a very brisk and busy fashion helps them to keep the ball straight. But others hit far too hard at the ball and lose control of the clubhead. They get, say, a 3 iron in their hands and feel that it's a 'power' club. So it is – if you have the hand action necessary for really excellent long-iron play.

However, it is possible to be effective with these clubs if you approach them with the same mental attitude as if playing just a firm mid-iron. Grip firmly, concentrate on swinging well within yourself and on making good contact, and let the length of shaft and lower flight give you distance.

My final message, however, is that if all else fails it's not sensible to persist. Play the percentages. A 3 iron not very badly mishit may only dribble along 120 yards or so. The same quality of strike with a 6 or 7 wood will produce a far better result for you.

I've played a few rounds recently with quite a long handicap player who can really make his 7-wood pay off. He used it as near the green as 120 yards and up to about 160. He hardly ever misses. Because he uses the club so often, he really knows it.

THE MID-IRONS

For me, these are the 5, 6, and 7 irons. With them, we are coming to the precision part of the game. As I've said, with your tee shot, whether it be with driver or 4-iron, you should be aiming for a specific area of fairway but not necessarily thinking in terms of a precise yard here or there. But these clubs are almost invariably struck into a green, with every player hoping to get the ball very near the hole indeed.

It's a matter of personal preference which club is the easiest in the set to play. Surely, however, the choice must lie amongst these three.

There are three main reasons why this is so:
1 The shafts are a much more manageable length.
2 Their increased loft reduces the amount of unintentional hook or slice spin.
3 We have yet to reach the extremes of loft which can result in a poor swing path sending the ball much higher and shorter than the player intended.

Certain differences now come into the golf swing. Power is of no real significance. There may be some excuse for thinking and boasting about how far you hit a drive or cracked a long iron but now, if you must boast, it should be about how near the flag you got your ball.

Some players begin to play with the ball pro-gressively further back in their stances, but I believe the ball should still be addressed just inside the front heel. The hands, however, be-cause of the shortening shaft will move in front of the clubhead, perhaps about opposite the middle of your front thigh.

The swing becomes slightly less sweeping, as it is with the woods and long irons, and you may naturally come to take more divot though less than with, say, a wedge.

Balance should not be changed, still about fifty-fifty distributed equally between the heels and balls of the feet.

Learn, either from experience and the look of the shot through the air how far you hit each club, or rely on pacing and yardages if you prefer. Try to learn a consistent *pace* of swing. Coldly decide from the evidence of practice what length of shot you will get from each club and maintain the same rhythm and balance. It's not how hard you hit the ball but how well that counts.

THE PITCHING CLUBS

These are the 8, 9, wedge and sand iron. For full shots the swing is very much the same as for the mid-irons. The difference results from the fact that you're standing closer to the ball. This, together with the shorter shaft, causes the back-swing and downswing to be on a steeper plane.

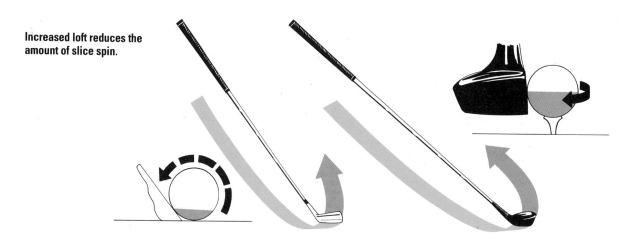

Increased loft reduces the amount of slice spin.

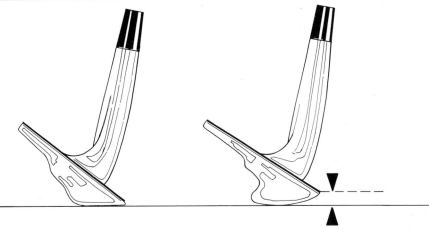

Right: Pitching wedge *left* and sand iron.

Below: With the shorter shaft of a mid-iron the hands will move in front of the clubhead. Still address the ball just inside the front heel.

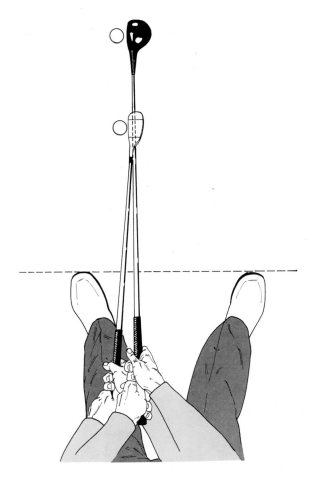

The ball remains just inside your front heel and the stance becomes narrower. Because one wants to hit down and through, set more weight on your front foot, say about 60 per cent.

A good many players prefer to open their stance as they see the shot very much as one played with hands and arms. It is very important that your knees are really relaxed. Greg Norman is a good example; at the end of his highly successful 1984 season he said to me, 'Peter, do you know why I've become so much more consistent with the short irons?' I said I'd noticed he wasn't hitting them as flat out as he used to. 'Yes,' he replied, 'that's true, but I've also learned to play with "soft" knees. It's given me a whole lot more rhythm and feel.'

So do remember that flowing movement below the waist is every bit as important in the short game as the long. The poor pitch shot is so often caused by a dead leg action, and that is why so many players push the ball out or cut it as well.

If that's your problem, think legs. It is also advisable to play from a fairly square stance as an open one makes a cutting shot more likely.

The amount of hand action is learned by trial and error. Some players seem to do little more than drop the clubhead on the ball. All the acceleration has come from the hands at the very last moment before impact. However, you do need to be in full practice or brimful of confidence to do this and doing it nearly all with the hands can

lead to inconsistency.

So far, I've not mentioned the sand iron. This is, or should be, the heaviest weapon in your armoury. It is seldom fully matched with the rest of your set, and being so heavy in the head is not really well suited to a swing at maximum power.

Think of it primarily as a precision club. It is possible to hit it 110 yards or so, as Tom Watson does, with full swing, but he only uses it this way for a special reason, such as playing over a bunker to a firm green with few yards to play with from that bunker to the flag. In that instance he wants the maximum stop that the sand iron can give. In general, though, use it just for shorter pitches, when you need the high flight and you have little ground to play with. You must keep the hands ahead of the clubhead or the rear of the flange may catch the turf and bounce your club into the ball.

Finally, it can be worth carrying two, even three wedges, as many tournament players do.

Far left: **Greg Norman's perfect stance for a pitch shot.**

Left: **Even though Watson is hitting a shot of probably only 110 yards, he still plays with a free-flowing action.**

Perhaps discard one of your woods or a long iron as they do – few carry more than two woods. If a particular player hits his wedge, say, 120 yards, and his sand iron 100, he may feel the need for a club that gives him 80 or 90 yards with a full swing. This is particularly true if he is happier pitching with a full swing. This additional wedge will have more loft and will perhaps be lighter and have a thinner leading edge.

Tom Kite, for instance, decided to make two of his long irons do the work of three by having the lofts altered. He credits some of his enormous money winnings and his great scoring consistency over recent years to having added a 'weak' wedge to his set.

THE SHORT PITCH

This is a shot played with anything from a sand iron up to an 8 (even a punch with a 6 to a very soft green). Most of the shot is through the air, with the rather gentle swing coming just from hands

and arms. There is only a slight body wind-up, just enough to preserve rhythm and balance.

I consider it the Achilles' heel of the vast proportion of club golfers, and many professionals too. Many reasonably talented players eventually achieve a fair competence with full-swing shots, bunker play, putting and chipping. In effect, they have learned the standard full golf swing, the specialized technique of bunker play, and shots where the clubhead travels only a very small proportion of the full swing distance. For them the short pitch swing lies in a kind of no man's land. The golfer that would be thoroughly disgusted at finishing only near the edge of a green with a full wedge shot has done far worse really if he fails to get his ball within one-putt distance with a pitch of between twenty and fifty yards.

There must be a reason for this weakness. What is it?

It is because many golfers see this shot as a scaling-down of a full shot with the same club. They are thinking in terms of making a gentler stroke at the ball and often a highly indecisive one.

Adopt a different approach. Think of more power, not less, and it will help you to play a crisper stroke.

This is how you set about it. Let's suppose you decide you want to pitch forty yards, the ball to run the remaining ten. Start with a mental picture of a shot with your wedge going just ten yards through the air. Build up from that to the feel needed for flight of forty yards. In this way, you'll be thinking of hitting more firmly than your first thought, not less.

You should hold the club down the grip, the stance open, feet only inches apart. With any increase from that ten yards starting point, use more shaft, broaden your stance progressively and, though it remains a hands and arms shot, allow more leg action and shoulder turn. Always think in terms of a nearly full swing with the club moving slowly.

For a short pitch, think in terms of a shot of just a few yards then mentally add power in small stages. It is basically a hands and arms shot, but allow more leg action and shoulder turn to achieve more distance.

CHIPPING
AND PUTTING

It has so often been said that the art or craft of putting is a 'game within a game'. Perhaps we could add chipping as well, because a chip is really just a long putt with the first few feet or yards of travel going through the air.
It makes sense to consider these two topics together because a fairly similar stroke is used for both and both are far removed from the full golf swing.

THE BASIC CHIP SHOT

Do you remember Seve Ballesteros 'chipping in' on the 18th at Wentworth against Arnold Palmer in the 1983 World Matchplay Championship? It was just about the shot of the year: a perfect stroke, like Tom Watson's 'chip-in' on the 71st hole at Pebble Beach in the 1982 US Open. Both led to dramatic victories.

I'm mentioning these two occasions because neither of these shots were technically chips at all and I want us to know what we're talking about. In fact, Ballesteros played a pitch and run from some sixty to seventy yards while Watson's shot was just a few yards from the hole. Surely that must have been a chip? Not so. Watson's ball was fairly well down and he played a high little cut lob.

Above: Only allow a small break in the wrists.

Left: The chip is played with a near pendulum movement.

Have a mental picture of the clubhead as an extension of the hand.

A true chip is really a very long lofted putt. The player should see it as a running shot. Depending on how lofted the club is the ball will be airborne initially but the player thinks in terms of his ball *running* at the hole after that first bit of loft.

A chip can be played with anything from a 4 iron to a sand wedge, though in the latter case the hands will be far ahead of the clubhead at impact and the ball well back in the stance, removing much of the loft.

All chip shots should mainly be played with the hands and arms with a sweeping pendulum movement. Although there should be some give in the wrists, they should break very little. Using a more wristy action leads to two things: more height on the shot and more chance of a disastrously heavy or thin chip. You can visualize the actual strike in two quite different ways. The first is the method I have always used. I like to feel that the clubhead is just an extension of my bottom hand and arm. This gives me the feeling that I am rolling the ball at the hole with the palm of my right hand, as in bowls. It gives you the feeling of the right hand and clubface acting as one. The clubface itself must be square to the target line until well after impact. Any tendency to let it roll over will lead to much inconsistency.

Other players like to feel that the clubhead is an extension of the back of their top hand. They feel that with this method their hands will be in front of the clubhead at impact. Arguably, this leads to rather more run on the ball than does my method, but both methods work admirably.

There is no reason why one should not think equally of both hands, if it works for you, but, as in putting, many golfers find it helpful to 'feel' the stroke in terms of one particular hand providing the pace or strike.

Always set slightly more weight on the front

69

foot. It helps to stop flicking and therefore hitting up at the ball. The clubhead path should either be level at impact or still moving ever so slightly downwards.

Most players find an open stance useful. It means the hips are cleared virtually before the stroke begins and this helps to allow hands and arms to swing through on the target line.

Have the ball quite close to the body. This leads to a straight up and down movement, but remember that you must still allow yourself enough room for the arms to swing freely.

Never take too short a backswing. A short backswing, especially at moments of crisis, leads to a tendency to jerk and flick at the ball. When it's very short, the player often comes to feel there just isn't enough pace in his swing and, at the last moment, forces the clubhead into the ball – almost always with the result that the shot is either hit

slightly thin or a divot is taken before the ball. However, there is another extreme. With a long backswing you must still accelerate into the ball. All chips, however short, must be struck crisply. If the clubhead is decelerating when it makes contact with the ball there is very little chance of chipping effectively.

As chipping requires just as much precise striking as putting, it helps to have the hands as close to the ball as possible. Place them towards the bottom of the grip. Now you can swing more firmly, which most players find helpful when playing this shot.

As for the grip, particularly if you're a very good putter, experiment with using your normal putting grip, for the short chip is very similar to a putt. But don't be too greedy. You are used to making a gentle stroke at the ball with your putting grip. If you use this grip from further and further away

from the green there may come a time when it stops working.

The chip stroke, if you have confidence in it, can be a saver from sand, if you've only twenty or thirty yards to go. Of course, you can use it only when the lip and face are very low indeed. The ball must be sitting cleanly and the sand firm. The ideal time is when the sand is wet. If you fail to take the ball first and then the sand, the result will be disastrous – you'll still be bunkered. Nip it away just as you would from a bare fairway lie.

As far as choosing the right club for chipping is concerned the rule-of-thumb is to select the club that will carry the ball the few feet onto the putting surface with the rest of its journey being run.

Obviously this means that you use straight-faced clubs when only just off the putting surface, the loft increasing as you get further away. This means, in theory, that you can go right through the irons from the number 1 to the sand wedge. according to the distance.

However, you must know exactly how the ball will behave from the clubface with every club. So most people should find it far easier to use no more than three clubs for chipping. On this basis, a good choice would be the 5, 7 and 9 irons, in each case employing the same standard stroke.

However, some players prefer to narrow the choice right down to just the one club, in this case usually a lofted one, the wedge or sand iron, perhaps. Better players can then vary the hand position for less or more run by hooding and closing the face for maximum run while having it square or open for short shots.

Playing the chip shot. The stance is a little open, the backswing not too short, and the ball struck crisply.

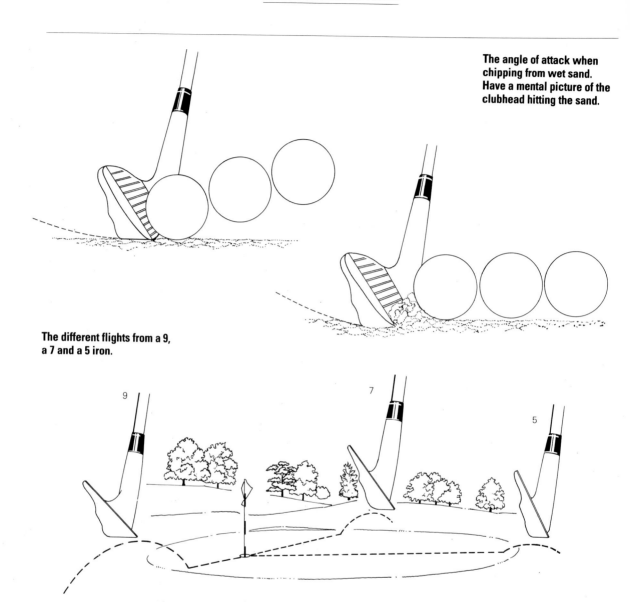

The angle of attack when chipping from wet sand. Have a mental picture of the clubhead hitting the sand.

The different flights from a 9, a 7 and a 5 iron.

All this requires manipulation with the hands and no standard stroke. A compromise is to specialize with, say, the 7. This will give you a little height from the clubface but there won't be much backspin so you'll always get a running shot. Finally, many quite good golfers are relatively poor chippers. If you are one of them, and after a lot of practice are still never fully confident with chipping, putt whenever you can. A moderate putt is always better than a poor chip.

PUTTING GRIPS

Many golfers have performed very well indeed on the greens with the same grip as they use for their other shots. In fact, I did myself, even when I had become a tournament player. However, one day the great Australian, Norman von Nida, looked my grip over in those early days when I used to putt quite well and pronounced that I would never be a really good putter unless I mended my ways.

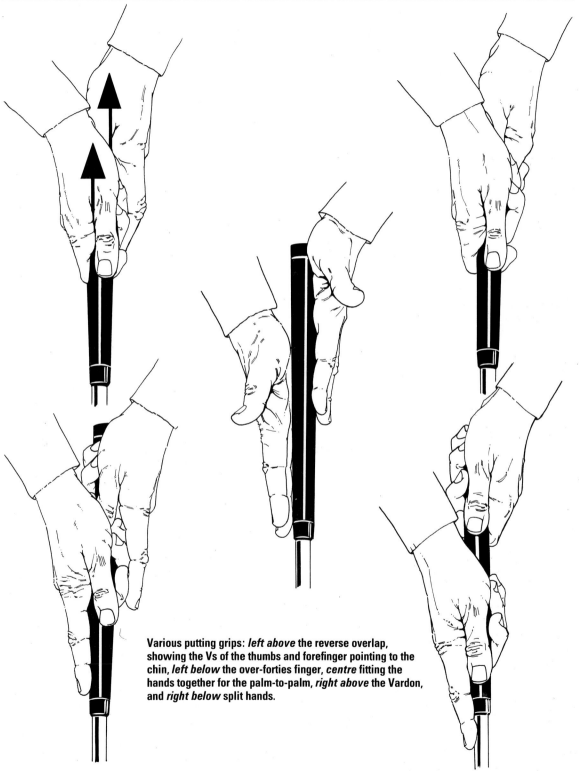

Various putting grips: *left above* the reverse overlap, showing the Vs of the thumbs and forefinger pointing to the chin, *left below* the over-forties finger, *centre* fitting the hands together for the palm-to-palm, *right above* the Vardon, and *right below* split hands.

Twenty-five years on – and my way of playing a chip shot hasn't changed since this picture was taken in 1961.

My left hand showed too many knuckles, he declared, and my right was too far over the top. Well, for three years and more Norman was unquestionably the star performer in British tournament golf and I was a fledgling. I did as he bade me and changed to the reverse overlap, used by 80 per cent of the best golfers today.

The reverse overlap most certainly didn't suit me. From that day to this I've missed more putts to the right than anyone else. Of course, I tried variations, for a while settling on the Byron Nelson version, with interlocking as well as the overlap. That did have its moments but I do so wish I'd stuck to that first grip. Everything about putting is highly personal so I suggest you stay with your own grip, however unorthodox, if it works.

The most popular putting grip is probably the Vardon. Although named after Harry Vardon, it was probably not originated by him but by Johnny Laidlay. The point of this grip is that it is in essence the standard golf grip (see pp. 12-14), but with the little finger of the bottom hand overlapping the forefinger of the top one.

The reverse overlap

However, most professionals seem to prefer the reverse overlap, as was recommended to me. There are two main features of this grip: the position of the hands on the club and the placing of the left forefinger. The back of the left hand (for right handers) and the palm of the right face the target. Normally, both thumbs go straight down the top of the shaft. If you check your grip in a mirror you will see that the Vs between thumb and forefinger of each hand point at the chin. All the fingers are on the club, which helps give more feel to the stroke, one of the essentials in putting.

The left forefinger is not on the shaft. Instead it is placed over the fingers of the right hand. It can either go between the little and third fingers, straight down or over other knuckles. Comfort is what counts. There are three main advantages of this position. The hands are brought closer together than in the Vardon grip; the top two fingers of the left hand automatically become more important; and the extension of the forefinger helps a player not to break the left wrist and push the putterhead in front of his hands, which is death to a consistent strike, as I know to my cost.

This grip was probably invented by the great American amateur, Walter Travis, early this century. Travis thought that it helped him to take the club back with the left hand and then to use the right hand in making his strike or tap at the ball. As Travis was universally recognized to be the greatest putter of his day his grip was naturally imitated. He taught it to Bobby Jones early in the 1920s and Walter Hagen also took it up at much the same time. Jones became one of the greatest approach putters of all time but, funnily enough, not an influence on putting styles. It was the drowsy rhythm of his driving and all full shots that captivated the world of golf. But with Hagen, it was quite another matter.

He was the Palmer or Ballesteros of the twenties and early thirties. Few thought to copy Walter Hagen for the long shots. He pushed, swayed and lunged and was expected to hit several bad ones per round, which he usually did. As a result he concentrated attention on his short game, and was masterful from 140 yards or so in. In his heyday, he was the supreme player of them all on the greens. He had tremendous nerve and confidence: once, with a putt to tie for the 1919 US Open, he summoned the leader from the clubhouse to watch him hole it (he did), and on another occasion, when complimented on holing a putt worth $2,000 (a lot of money those days) he

retorted: 'What? Miss a putt for $2,000? Not likely!' Small wonder that *his* putting grip was copied.

Palm to palm

I'd be the last to argue the reverse overlap should be the one and only. As I grew up as tournament player, Bobby Locke was the supreme champion. For the long game he felt he modelled himself on Jones. He certainly had the rhythm and balance if not technique. For putting he once sat at the feet of Walter Hagen. However, although Locke later credited Hagen with much of his supreme success as a putter, he used a different grip. The reverse overlap made his grip for other shots feel uncomfortable. For Locke, then, it was the Vardon grip, as in the rest of his game – but a little modified. He moved the left hand under the shaft so that his thumb was nearly straight down, with the back of the hand facing the hole. So also for the right hand – palm on line of stroke to the hole. Basically then, Locke's grip was similar to that of such modern masters as Watson, Ballesteros and Faldo, but he overlapped the right little finger while they extend the left forefinger.

This palm-to-palm grip is the one I strongly recommend for all players, with the overlapping of the fingers left to personal choice and feel. I'm sure the feeling of having the back of the left hand and the palm of the right travelling back and towards the hole is a great help. A minor modification is to have the right forefinger much further down the shaft than for the full swing. The great Gene Sarazen christened this the 'over-forties finger' and had it straight down so that his right wrist tightened up and added impetus through the ball.

In my own career, I had spells of putting with my hands reversed, much as Bernhard Langer does for the short ones today. Arnold Palmer is also among the many who have experimented with this grip. In my own case, I putted much better with it from 1965 and had four very good years which made me a big winner. Alas, I was tempted to use it for longer and longer putts. In the end it all went and in 1969 I reached an all-time low in putting.

It was quite effective for short putts but I found I lacked feel from longer distance. They used to say to me: 'You're just like your dear old father. He couldn't put them in a bucket either.'

However, there were those good years so if you have really horrid problems on the greens do give this grip a try. It makes putting rather a left-hand, back-hand stroke, with the putterhead being pulled towards the hole, but it does prevent the left wrist breaking before the ball is struck.

All the grips I've discussed help keep the hands close together but a few players have been successful setting the hands well apart. Nearly twenty years ago, for instance, the illustrator of one of my earlier books, *Easier Golf*, achieved temporary fame. Paul Trevillion wasn't even a golfer but, putting with his right hand just inches from the bottom of the shaft, challenged the world to beat him at holing out from 3 feet. No one took him on so we shall never know how infallible he might have proved to be.

In more recent years, the former US Open Champion, Hubert Green, has been one of the best putters in the world. In his case, the hands are just a couple of inches or so apart. Both these variants, of course, help to make the right hand the dominant partner in the putting stroke. The left does little more than just steady the club. Denis Durnian, who recorded that incredible 28 for the first nine holes during the 1983 British Open, has a similar method. His hands are apart but he places the right forefinger down the shaft.

Some have gone even further, using the right hand only. It worked for one of the Turnesa brothers – but for a while only. I've also been told of a real oddity. That great English soccer inside forward of the post-war era, Len Shackleton, uses a conventional grip for golf except for the really vital putts. Then he putts with just the right hand on the club. He says he'd do it all the time but he suffers from a kind of tennis elbow and it hurts too much. Is this cowardice or common sense?

Perhaps if he used it all the time, that special magic ingredient would wear off.

Eduardo Blasi, an Argentine golfer of some thirty years ago, had an interesting variation. He tried a one-handed grip, with a putter only 18 inches long. He rested his left hand on his left knee and had his right hand well down the shaft. It all caused quite a stir at the time – until they noticed he was truly hopeless!

The most famous example, however, of a great player who used an unorthodox approach must be Samuel Jackson Snead. After a tremendous, long career at the top, he began to suffer from dreadful nerves on the short ones. Having tried just about everything, Sam decided to putt between his legs. Using a centreshaft, he placed his left hand at the top of the grip, with the thumb pressing on top. The right hand was well down the shaft and pushed through towards the target. The nervous twiches went and the method was quite effective, especially for short and medium-length putts. He had given hope to thousands!

However, those stern custodians of tradition, the US Golf Association and the Royal and Ancient Golf Club of St Andrews, banned the method. It certainly wasn't elegant and they felt it wasn't in keeping with the true traditions of the game. But Snead was a resourceful fellow. He kept much of his method but positioned the ball outside his right foot with both of his feet still pointing towards the hole, the right almost behind the left.

He was back in business.

GRIP PRESSURE

How tightly should the putter be held? Well, great players have varied very widely indeed. Bobby Locke, for example, said that the club should be held only firmly enough to prevent it falling out of the hands. As light a grip as possible increased his feel of the clubhead and meant that all his muscles were relaxed. Locke believed that he had exceptionally sensitive fingers and that a firm grip made them less so. On the other hand Tom Watson – one of the best pressure putters at short range of modern times – has a very firm grip indeed but his touch doesn't seem impaired. Watch him on long and medium-length putts. His ball almost always finishes just a foot or so past the hole (and, of course, drops in often). That rigid-looking quick push at the ball still manages to contain feel, not, I suspect, from the hands but from the upper arm. Seve Ballesteros has wrists, arms and shoulders all working together and is very nearly his equal but perhaps not quite as convincing at the vital three and a half to five foot distance. Seve holds the club just as lightly as Bobby Locke. His right forefinger is limp and he crouches over the ball. With Seve, it all looks very much a matter of touch and feel. Henry Cotton and Neil Coles played for a phase gripping the club as if to strangle it. Both found it helped beat a putting twitch.

If these examples don't give a clear message,

Sam Snead's sidesaddle putting style.

that is because so many things in putting depend, at the end of the day, on what works for you.

My own opinion is that there should be two pressures. Grip lightly on long putts when the aim is to get the feel of the strength of stroke required to run the ball near to the hole. However, when you are sufficiently near to be confident that a three-putt is not a danger you need a firm, decisive stroke. This is much more likely to be achieved if you have a firm – but not tightly clenched – grip on your putter. (Never let tightness into your forearms.) Without that firm grip, the head of your putter may waver and strike the ball slightly open or closed. There is also more chance of body movement.

Tommy Armour won the 1931 British Open Championship at Carnoustie needing a putt of just over three and a half feet to do so. Next day, the great golf writer Bernard Darwin, commented in

The Times that he'd never seen a putt to win a great championship holed with so much nonchalance. Years later, Armour commented that he had suddenly changed the grip he'd used in the whole championship and also stiffened up because he was paralysed with terror. He didn't even see his clubhead strike the ball. how different the observer's view from the actual player's!

BALL AND HEAD POSITION

Have the ball opposite your front foot and your head either vertically above the ball or just fractionally behind it. It is true that people have putted well with the ball well away from their body or well towards the middle of their stance and even off the back foot, but I cannot think of an example where either of these has worked for very long. If these positions do regularly work well for you, then

Below left: There are many variations on playing the straight putt, but the main thing to consider is alignment and feeling comfortable.

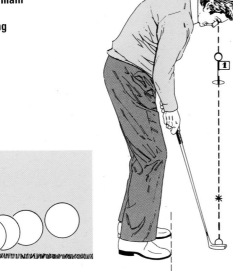

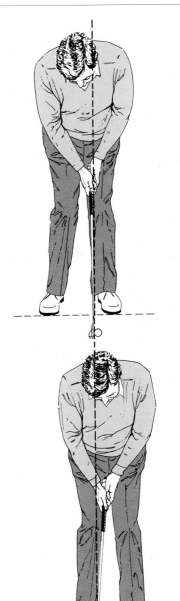

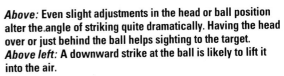

Above: Even slight adjustments in the head or ball position alter the angle of striking quite dramatically. Having the head over or just behind the ball helps sighting to the target.
Above left: A downward strike at the ball is likely to lift it into the air.

don't feel you have to change, but if they lose their effectiveness the sheer mechanics could be the problem.

Once you have the ball well back in your stance, a downward strike at the ball becomes more likely, something I must admit worked for one great putter, Lloyd Mangrum. If it lies well away from you, you can't possible have your head over the ball.

Having your head over the ball, or just behind it, is a great help in sighting along the line to the target and helps to give the feeling of hitting the ball *away*, something that Jack Nicklaus, for one, considers useful if not essential.

A forward ball position helps one to hit with less backspin. Many players used to think that topspin sent the ball on its way, until scientists eventually showed this could not be so. However, although you will not get topspin, the ball will roll more freely, enabling you to putt more gently. Certainly, the further a ball rolls on a long putt with little effort from the player, the better. Obviously, the harder you hit a long putt, the more you lose sense of touch.

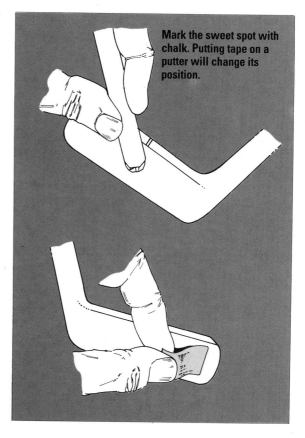

Mark the sweet spot with chalk. Putting tape on a putter will change its position.

EXACT STRIKING

Many club golfers do not realize how important it is to bring the 'sweet spot' of the putter into contact with the equator of the ball. All, of course, notice quickly enough when they stub the turf before the ball or sometimes, usually on a long putt, half top the ball, but many quite good golfers merely think of lining the face of their putter square to the hole with the ball against the middle. Sometimes, you will be all right but the sweet spot is seldom right in the middle of the head.

Finding it is a pretty simple matter. Take any golf ball you like, though a high-compression one works best, and bounce it on the blade. Start at the centre and work towards the heel (you will virtually never find the spot towards the toe). When you've found it there will be no vibration in your putter shaft. Having made your discovery, make a nick on the top of your putterhead and

always aim to bring that spot on the putter into contact with the middle of the ball. Walter Hagen in practice used to put a chalk mark on the sweet spot. All was well if it quickly disappeared.

If you find the sweet spot is too much towards the heel for your taste and want it in the middle, you can move it quite simply. Stick lead tape towards the toe end. After each short strip, note the changed position of the sweet spot and you will eventually have it in the middle of the blade. There is only one disadvantage in this procedure. With each strip you will be making the clubhead heavier and will not rejoice if you prefer a light putter head!

My father discussed this subject with Walter Hagen and I've talked to Bobby Locke, Bob Charles and Tom Watson, amongst many. Those are four of the very best putters ever, and are all unanimous on the vital importance of exact striking.

If you still doubt the importance of finding the sweet spot, when watching television see how tournament players, perhaps facing a putt of thirty yards, seem able to take a short backswing and swing slowly and gently, with little or no follow-through. The actual strike is so perfect that the ball runs on and on. For the same length of putt, some handicap players seem to take a big enough swing for an 8 iron pitch, yet the ball, not struck properly, still comes up short.

PUTTING METHODS

Of course, there are many ways of putting. I should know. I must have tried out most of them during my tournament career!

I was, and still am, fascinated by putting technique, probably because the long game came fairly easily to me. I had far less incentive to see how the rest did it.

Although I have studied the methods of the masters, I would not recommend them all to you. For example, I've never seen a better putter than the great South African Bobby Locke, but he was just about impossible to imitate. Few, I fear, would benefit from his method of standing well away from the ball, swinging the club back around the right heel, allowing himself quite an amount of body movement, and finishing with no follow-through. Another South African, Gary Player, was almost his equal. He earned his reputation as a great bunker expert who was often able to get down in two from sand largely because of his splendid holing-out. Even so, I cannot recommend the Player method either. For most of his career, Gary has used a jabbing stroke, feet close together in a shut stance, the backswing short and, again, no follow-through. Few could emulate him and still have very good feel for distance.

If you look around you, you'll find that most of the people who putt best at your own golf club have a method that's very much their own. It may look very strange indeed, but even so, you can be sure that it's the result of much thought and experimentation. You have to think about the way

you play and try different methods to improve your putting. Watch the good putters on TV. Try to see what basics they have in common and how they differ. Do the same at your own club.

Billy Casper

Most of the good putters of the past employed a 'wristy' stroke. By this, I mean that they took the club back with the hands and let the wrists break freely; the arms only really came into the stroke on longer putts.

It's a method that finds very little favour today, on account of one inherent problem: it's quite easy to allow the putter head to reach the ball before the hands are directly over the top of it. This makes for poor striking and inconsistent length and direction.

Yet the wristy Billy Casper ranks with the greatest putters ever, so there must be something right with his method. He believes himself

Billy Casper

Bob Charles makes it look oh so simple.

that the natural geometry of the wrist is a great aid to good putting, and says that if you grip the club with the back of your top hand facing the target and the palm of your bottom, then the hingeing action of the wrists that follows is perfectly along the intended line of putt.

Well, I think this is valid and certainly worth trying. To avoid letting the clubhead get ahead of the hands, perhaps have the ball in mid-stance as the great Australian Jim Ferrier did, another superb – and wristy – putter.

Bob Charles

Here we move to the other extreme from Casper. The tall New Zealander believes that there should be no wrist action at all in the stroke. He sees it as a pendulum movement, centred, he says, at the base of the neck.

Essentially, Bob Charles's stroke comes from the shoulders. As this involves using large muscles, and therefore less sensitive ones, the effect of nerves ought to be lessened. Nevertheless, Bob himself admits to having twitched a few in the last two or three years – somehow, though, they don't seem to me to be very bad twitches as these horrors go, but he can feel an involuntary movement when others can't see one.

If your own method is at all like Bob's, I'd suggest that the thought you might learn the most from is his belief that the putting action should stem from the base of the neck. A fringe benefit is that this helps you to keep a still head.

Alf Padgham

Now here's a name from the past. Until he was nearly thirty years old, Alf was rather a poor putter but an excellent chipper, two arts that are often very closely allied. He was then inspired to try to putt like he chipped. Lo and behold, it worked! For a while, he carried all before him, including a spell of four consecutive wins and the British Open of 1936.

His new method meant that Alf broke one or two of the golden rules of putting. No, he most definitely didn't have his head over the top of the

The Padgham method

ball and his eyes behind the line. Obviously, he had the ball much further away from his body than normal and also an open stance – again his position when chipping.

However, the great advantage to Padgham, and perhaps others, was that he was able to include something he was very good at, the chipping stroke, into his putting style. Putting became 'natural' for him. Most of the best putters have, for me, always seemed to make this devilish art look just that, and I have never seen a good putter look uncomfortable.

Lee Trevino

Here's a man that's never, to my knowledge, spoken of as a great putter. Undeniably, however, he has been renowned for having very hot spells with the blade. His putting and chipping during his British Open wins of 1971 and 1972 defied belief at times. Even in 1984, he still looked a highly able performer and proved it by winning the US PGA when nearing the age of forty-five.

As regards putting and chipping, he is – as in the rest of his golf swing – very left-side-dominated. To Trevino, a putt is a stroke hit with the back of his top hand, the left in his case.

Most who have talked to me about putting feel that the bottom hand, for nearly all of them the right, gives 'feel' to the stroke. Trevino is an interesting exception and a man who has superb feel for the pace and run of a putt. If you play racket games left handed but golf right, or vice versa, the Trevino method is worth serious attention. After all, there've been many tennis players far stronger on the backhand side. It may not apply to the full golf swing but putting obeys few rules . . .

Diegling

Once, long ago, they were all doing it, at much the same time as the Charleston was enjoying its greatest vogue. Leo Diegel, one of the greatest improvisational shot-makers the game has seen, was also one of the most nervous. For his problems on the greens, very severe, Leo devised what you might call the 'opposed elbows' method. A right-hander, he pointed his left elbow at the target and his right directly away from it. The feel he wanted was of both elbows flowing along a straight line, no wrists or hands in the stroke. He used a long shafted putter, so long that his hands were quite close to his chin.

In some ways, as regards the arms, this is the Bob Charles method. It produces a most definite pivoting from the base of the neck. It made Leo

Lee Trevino

The Diegel method.

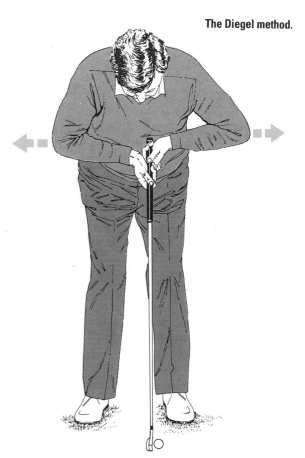

a deadly short putter – when the pressure wasn't on – but reduced his feel for distance on longer putts. When the pressure *was* on, he wasn't any too good from short range either.

However, that was Leo's particular problem. In the whole history of golf, no one has thrown more major championships away through failure of nerve on the greens. Walter Hagen knew it well. When both were staying at the Marine Hotel in North Berwick during the 1929 Open at Muirfield, Hagen was gently chided for lingering too long before going to bed. Leo Diegel, they said, leader by a clear two strokes, had long since gone. Said Hagen: 'Yeah, but he ain't sleeping. Your deal.' Leo reached the turn in 43 the following morning . . .

Even so, I think his strange putting method is worth consideration. Mechanically, he was on the right lines and solved the problem of lack of touch on the long ones by carrying a second, heavier, putter. You might also care to try out his idea of very frequently beginning a round with a *new* putter. He had that necessary optimism about putting which told him that a new dawn, a new club might reveal all. However, he didn't expend as much cash as you might think with this notion. A quick paint job on the shaft or putterhead of an old club was all that was needed to give it the necessary 'new' look and feel.

Ben Crenshaw

We are now talking about a man whom many copy. Like Padgham, he stands open, arms well away from the body but, unlike Padgham's, Crenshaw's action is wristless and hinged at the shoulders. It is another classic style.

If there's been a real major change in golf technique since I started out myself, it's probably in putting. The wristy style is rare today, and not a few putting strokes indeed look very much a carbon copy of Crenshaw's.

Another point to note as regards Ben is that, in contrast to Diegel, he has kept the same putter all through his career from about the age of fifteen, though I dare say there's been the occasional

Ben Crenshaw

experiment. Outstanding putters do seem to stick to the same club, and such people perhaps blame off days or spells on themselves or the putting surface, while the rest of us tend to keep on the search to find that one club which will solve all our problems.

Tom Watson

A fellow tournament professional said of Tom: 'If we all missed all of the greens, Tom Watson would win every tournament.'

He wasn't speaking just of Watson's putting, of course. The man from Kansas City was, in my opinion, the finest there was at 'getting it up and down in two' from within fifteen to twenty yards of the green.

Of course, he had a brilliant variety of shots up to fifty yards. Nevertheless, it was his putting that impressed me the most.

When one watches Watson, one isn't immediately aware of a man with masterful touch at

Tom Watson

the way he unerringly rattled them in when that elbow angle remained constant – and from a range of about five yards! No mean feat, I can tell you. He could do it a dozen times without glancing at the line again!

If you have a reverence for statistics, you might like to note that Tom always performs well in the USA PGA lists for lowest average putts per round. He usually manages to keep his US Tour average between 28 and 29. How standards have changed! Once, that would most definitely have been considered an almost miraculous figure for *one* round.

Jack Nicklaus

No awards for Jack as regards putting statistics. Where he scores is in, as they say, 'greens in regulation'. Yet Nicklaus, for my money, is still a very remarkable putter indeed.

Jack Nicklaus　　　　　　　　　*Right:* **Arnold Palmer**

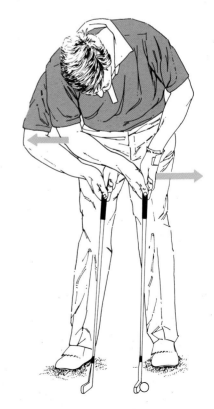

work – as, for instance, with Seve Ballesteros. He looks to hold the putter far more firmly than the norm and his right hand is in a very strong, and high-arched position. This may well help to 'lock' his right elbow through the stroke, which would help make it consistent.

While many people have talked of the importance of the left wrist, Watson is more concerned with the elbow. He tries to maintain his address position through the stroke, believing that 'breaking' the elbow on the backswing makes the arc of the stroke unreliable. (Back to Diegel?) If he has a spell of, for him, poor putting, he first works on that part of the stroke. Watson demonstrated his thoughts clearly during our BBC Pro-Celebrity series at Gleneagles in 1983 when he showed how he missed putts when he varied the angle of his left elbow. However, I was even more impressed by

Through both my playing and commentating career, I can think of no one who can compare at holing putts when they're really needed.

Do you remember the classic finish of the 1977 Turnberry Open? The cause was lost, with Watson, a stroke in hand, no more than a couple of feet from the hole but Nicklaus holed from the front of the green, perhaps eighteen yards. All right, he still lost by a single stroke but didn't he go down with guns blazing!

I can remember a turning point that rested on putting during Nicklaus's 1980 US Open victory. First, from rather a long distance, he left his approach putt almost laughably short. But the eyes grew steely, he screwed up his nerve – and got the next one in.

Though nerve is such an important feature of Nicklaus's game both on and off the green, his method has one or two lessons that may be useful for ordinary mortals.

One, I think, is the piston-like movement of the right arm, sliding back and down the line. His action is very much a right handed one. Another is that he also crouches fairly low and gets his head behind the ball, looking along the line to the hole – very different from Padgham's and Crenshaw's methods.

Although I have always much criticized slow play, I was impressed by a remark Jack once made to me. 'Any ninety shooter can miss 'em quickly.' So Jack has always been very deliberate indeed, although he has speeded up a little in recent years. In the past he used to, as he said, 'Have to wait until I felt ready.'

Psychologically, that's not as easy to do as you might think. There may be a voice inside telling you how foolish you'll look if you miss it badly after taking so long over it.

CHOOSING A PUTTER

Although it's so often been said that putting is a game within a game, I don't agree. I'd call it two: approach putting and holing out. The first requires getting the ball reasonably on line but more

important requirements are judgment and touch. Of course, we all want to hole out but it's much more sensible from twenty yards to be trying to get the ball within three feet of the hole in order to hit it in next shot.

The other game within a game, holing out, is rather a different animal. In the three and a half to five feet range, judgment and touch are much less important. Often, just one apparently simple question is asked: Can I hit the ball exactly on the line I've chosen?

It would make a lot of sense to carry two putters. Many indeed have. Why not, indeed, three (the extra one being for the medium-length putts). However, the Rules of Golf allow us a total of only fourteen clubs, and in order not to cramp the style too much in other quite important parts of the game, most golfers have come to feel that just one putter will have to do. Yet we have to putt on both slow and fast greens, flat or heavily contoured, broad-bladed meadow grass or the finest fescues. Some players combat the variations by hitting off the toe when greens are fast while moving the ball back in their stance when they're slow. 'Hit it', they say, 'off the heel when you've a right-to-left putt (for right handers) and off the toe for a left-to-right.'

All golfers have tried out a great variety of putters, even if it was just for two or three strokes on the practice green. We are all seeking the magic wand. It's quite remarkable, however, that many of the players with legendary powers on the greens have settled on one *type* of putter, though not necessarily always the same model. Jack Nicklaus, for instance, has always favoured a blade. It was therefore strange to see him using a Ping in the first round at the 1981 British Open at Royal St George's. It was perhaps, then not so strange that he went on to amass a total of 83. The next day he appeared with his familiar blade and knocked seventeen strokes off that horrific first-round score.

It is useful, then, to see what the great putters in the history of golf, past and present, use, or have used.

Isao Aoki	*Centreshaft*. Coke hammer shape with a spiky toe. Much experimentation in weighting with lead tape.
George Archer	*Ping*. A US Tour winner in 1984 in his mid-forties. At his peak in the late 1960s they used to say one of the best ever seen.
Seve Ballesteros	*Ping*. While many use a Ping because it's rather forgiving for the putt not quite hit out of the sweet spot, Seve uses one because he says he finds it the easiest to line up.
Jerry Barber	*Heel centreshaft*. Almost always outhit from the tee, he once had a sequence over the last three holes of putts from forty, forty and sixty feet to tie for the 1959 US PGA.
Deane Beman	*Centreshaft Bull's Eye*. Another short hitter, who is now the US Tour's commissioner, who made up the leeway on the greens.
Michael Bonallack	*Centreshaft, 'Golden Goose'*. He works on the principle that you must will the putts into the hole.
Ken Bousfield	*Blade*. The best teacher I ever had on the short game. Always took the club back slowly.
Harry Bradshaw	*Blade with hickory shaft*. Believed in keeping the head down and listening for the ball to drop.
Ken Brown	*Rusty blade with short hickory shaft*. Uses other putters but this one re-appears. It's his trade mark.
José-Maria Canizares	*Ping*. Arguably, year in and year out, the best putter on the European Tour.

Billy Casper	*D-shaped mallett*. Ben Hogan once unkindly said to him: 'If you couldn't putt you'd be selling hot dogs outside the ropes.'
Bob Charles	*Centreshaft*. His superb putting used to obscure the steadiness of the rest of his game. Making a huge mark on the US Senior Tour.
Bruce Crampton	*Mallett*. The best player of the last twenty years not to win a major championship.
Ben Crenshaw	*Blade with rear flange*. The best present-day putter, perhaps, with his Wilson 8802.
Nick Faldo	*Ping*. Has also played with a Crenshaw-type putter but at best with a Ping.
Ray Floyd	*Ping, mallett and Zebra*. Floyd is less faithful than most. In his case, his stance (very upright) and length of shaft (about three inches more than normal) are more important.
Doug Ford	*Mallett with hickory shaft*. His ability on the greens and from sand enabled him to more than hold his own with otherwise more talented players.
David Graham	*Centreshaft*. Does vary, however.
Hubert Green	*Old blade*. Spread hands technique.
Walter Hagen	*Blade with hickory shaft*. A great believer in the sweet spot.
Harold Henning	*Centreshaft*. Came close to winning the 1983 Open when nearing fifty.
Ben Hogan	*Heel centreshaft*. The shaft was set more towards the heel than standard.

Tony Jacklin	*Ping.* But has tried a host of others.
Bobby Jones	*Blade with hickory shaft.* He called it 'Calamity Jane'. Twine was used on two repairs to the shaft, and appeared as features on manufactured copies!
Gene Littler	*Mallett, Ping, Centreshaft and Basakwerd.* Always looks natural whatever he's using.
Bobby Locke	*Blade with hickory shaft.* The shaft was extra long and the lie rather flat. The best putting club I've ever picked up.
Nancy Lopez	*Mallett.* One of the best putters in women's golf.
Lloyd Mangrum	*Mallett.* Deadly from six feet down.
Graham Marsh	*Centreshaft.* Experiments with others.
Johnny Miller	*Centreshaft.* Always used one in his halcyon days. Changed to a blade but has since returned.
Jack Nicklaus	*Blade with flange.* A few experiments.
Alf Padgham	*Blade with long yellow shaft.* A beautifully balanced club, and he seemed to hole everything for a few years.
Arnold Palmer	*Everything under the sun.* But used a blade 90 per cent of the time in his great years.
Gary Player	*Blade.* This was a Jack Nicklaus model that he bought for $50 in Japan many years ago.
Bill Rogers	*Mallett.* Quite an old club.
Bob Rosburg	*Blade.* With his superb touch he can use anything.
Sam Snead	*Blade and centreshaft.* Used a blade in his heyday but centreshaft suits his side-saddle style.
Peter Thomson	Not a sentimentalist, I believe he used a different putter in each of his championship victories. One I recall was a long hickory-shaft, given him by Norman von Nida.
Walter Travis	*Centreshaft.* Called a Schenectady, it may have caused this form of putter to be banned by the R & A for many years. Although Travis is said to be the inventor of the centreshaft, in fact he borrowed one when his putting was off in practice for the 1904 Amateur at Sandwich, which he won.
Lee Trevino	*Blade.* At his best with this kind of putter though there've been many experiments.
Tom Watson	*Ping.* Almost invariably 'gave the hole a chance'.
Tom Weiskopf	*Blade.* Changed occasionally and liked a long shaft.

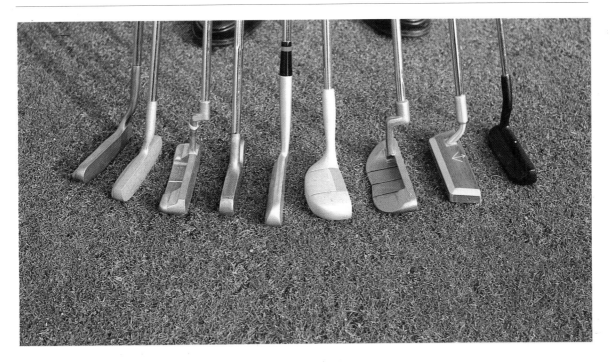

What lessons can we learn? Well, for a start, none of my great putters is really eccentric in his choice. Obviously, blades, centreshafts, Pings and malletts lead the field. Although a few players can putt with anything, most settle for a single type of putter.

You may have noticed, however, that not a few are insistent that the shaft should be above standard length. This is because they wish to stand upright, and to get the greater feel of the clubhead given by the extra length.

Many have also experimented with finding exactly the weight that suits them, using lead tape for fine adjustments.

The essentials in choosing a putter can perhaps be narrowed down to two. You should be able to feel that you can line it up square to the target, and it should immediately feel right when you pick it up. Alas, feel can alter from one day to another and clubs that feel right when you swing them in the pro's shop or factory do not feel at all the same when you actually strike a golf ball with them.

I suggest that a fairly heavy putter is more suited to the majority of players and courses. A

A minute selection of the putters available.

light one seems to waver on the backstroke, especially in wind, and you do have to hit just that little bit harder. The body tends to move as a result and you may mis-hit. With the heavier head you can putt a little more gently and always feel where the head is.

I have picked up Bobby Jones's famous 'Calamity Jane' in the US Golf Association museum in Far Hills, New Jersey. What a frightener it was. The head was as light as a toothpick and was extremely lofted by modern standards. No doubt he found the extra loft useful because the greens were so much poorer in his day, but he must have had a very delicate touch to feel that clubhead.

Another putter I've tried, just as famous, is Bobby Locke's. In this case, my feelings were very different. The club seemed to want to swing back and return to the ball correctly. There was no torque or whip. It was ideal and the grain impeccably straight, a Stradivarius amongst putters.

In conclusion one comes back to putting being really two games, not one. A long shaft and an erect stance help feel on long putts, especially when combined with a relatively heavy head. For the short ones, practically the reverse is true. Most players seem to benefit from crouching, going down the shaft and giving the ball a short, sharp jab.

READING A GREEN

Far more than is often realized, being able to read a green will only come from experience. Your beginner may often be able to strike a putt reasonably well and straight, but is seldom dead from long distance. He's just not learned to judge the run of the ball or have an eye for distance.

Once that eye for distance and pace has been developed I think that much of the green pacing and estimating of line makes little real difference. A good player can see all he needs to know in just a few seconds.

However, extra time taken does have benefits. For some, it helps the concentration or allows the nerves to settle, especially in tournament play. You may find a little more time (but do make it seconds not minutes) helps to confirm your first thoughts.

You will learn from experience whether you need to look over a putt both from behind the ball and from behind the hole. Viewing from the side can help some get better feel of distance.

The grain of the grass can make a great deal of difference to the roll of the ball, and there's a well-known rule of thumb to help you. A shiny appearance, though noticeable only on sunny days, as you look along the line of putt to the hole means the grass is growing in that direction, and a greener and darker look means it is against you. The first putt will be much faster than the second. If you are putting across the grain, this will be revealed by views from the side of your line.

A look inside the hole can show in which direction the last cut was made. The worn out side will show the direction of cut, with roots exposed.

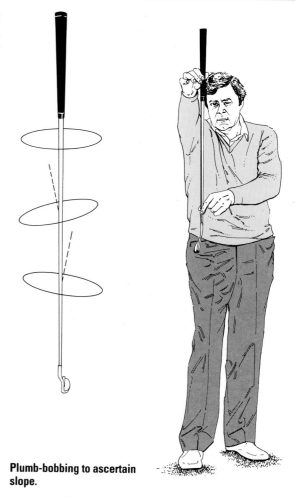

Plumb-bobbing to ascertain slope.

Local knowledge can also be useful, especially on a hilly course, and may be worth a casual question from a visiting player. The grass can grow either towards the rising sun or the setting, and will usually grow towards water and away from hill slopes.

A fairly severe cross slope won't have very much effect on a wet winter green where the grass has been allowed to grow considerably beyond its competition length. However, if the grain is with you on close-cut greens what a difference can result . . .

You should not discount the influence of the wind. It really does speed the pace of a fast downhiller alarmingly at times, and the borrow of a putt also. Keep your wits about you. Don't ground your putter in case the ball moves. There's no penalty stroke on the greens just for planting your feet. Plumb-bobbing is one method for seeing whether there is any borrow. You allow your putter to dangle free between thumb and forefinger at arm's length, between your eye, ball, possible slope and the hole. If there's no slope, the putter shaft will appear to be perpendicular. If there is one, the shaft will slant in the direction of slope. Well, it sounds easy but I preferred to rely on my feel for pace and line. That, if not the ability to knock the short ones in, just came naturally.

The darker the grass, the slower the putt. The 16th green at Augusta.

BUNKER
TECHNIQUES

It has always been my contention that bunker (sand trap) play is
easy, except from those few lies that really are difficult, or even
downright impossible.

By 'easy' I don't mean to suggest that all of us should be able to
hole out from a greenside bunker fairly frequently and lay the rest
dead. Nor that, with much longer bunker play, a precision shot is
particularly easy. However, no competent player should fear any
standard sand shot. All that is usually needed is a little thought
before you start.

FAIRWAY BUNKERS

The secrets of the successful shot from a fairway bunker depend on your lie, the depth of the bunker, the height and steepness of the face and, most important of all, how precise a striker you are. One of the most famous golf shots of all was a long iron played from loose blown sand by Bobby Jones to the 71st green at Royal Lytham in the 1926 British Open, a championship-winning stroke if ever there was one. In fact, there was no extreme magic in it. Jones was lying quite well, probably on sandy ground rather than in a bunker, but nipped the ball clean and with extreme precision. It was the critical point of the championship, and it is the occasion on which it was played rather than the shot itself that has made the achievement resound down the years.

The good club golfer has to weigh up the situation and the possibilities of success and disaster, and look at his own abilities with a cold clear eye. If you've been hitting long irons and woods a touch heavy all through the round, the odds are stacked high against your suddenly being able to whip a similar shot clean from sand. What is far more likely is that your clubhead will die in the sand and your ball will be moved only a few yards, perhaps ending in a far worse position under the bunker face. However, if you've no face to contend with, and an expanse of fairway ahead, by all means take as straight-faced a club as you like. But don't wiggle your feet down too deeply for this shot, as it can take you below the level of the ball increasing the chances of a heavy shot.

Plant your feet firmly, however, otherwise you won't be able to make the pivot essential to hitting any good long shot. Thereafter, make a normal good swing at the ball, perhaps shortening both your grip and backswing a trifle to increase your control. This will make good ball contact more likely.

If you have a tendency to slice, you are more likely to do so on this shot. Make allowance by aiming off.

Let's suppose next that you have a good lie,

roughly in the middle of the bunker with a face, though not a severe one, to clear in front. What club, you ask yourself, shall I use for maximum length while feeling confident I'll clear the face? Practice and experience are the best guides but, for most club golfers, experience alone has to provide the answer. Golf clubs often have a practice greenside bunker but seldom a fairway one. However, here's a tip you may find useful. Look at the angle of the face of the bunker and compare it with the angle of loft on the club you're thinking of using. If they look much the same, use a more lofted club, going for example from a 5 to a 7 iron.

However, even if there's only a moderately severe face confronting you, your first aim should be to get back to the fairway. Perhaps try to make a little extra distance, using a 9 or 8 iron. When in doubt, think of Johnny Miller playing the last hole of the 1975 Open Championship at Carnoustie

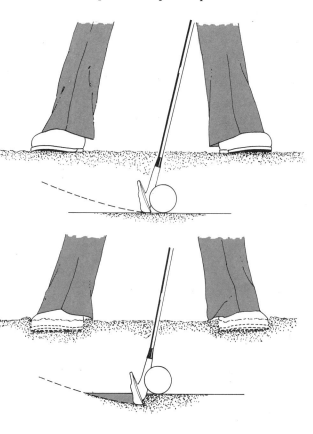

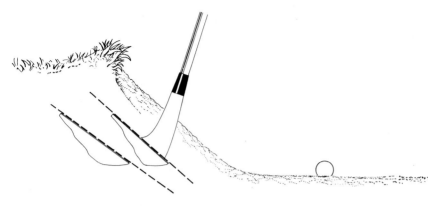

Using a club with a greater angle of loft than the angle on the bunker face will help you clear it.

bunkered to the right of the fairway. He needed a par to beat his playing partner Jack Nicklaus and give himself a chance of a tie with players still out on the course. Miller calculated that it had to be a 6 iron to reach the green. Well, he did so – but only after he had left his first attempt in the sand. I'm not suggesting that Miller was being foolhardy on this occasion. It was a calculated risk when all was already nearly lost, the sort of risk worth taking, perhaps, in a similar position in a Sunday morning fourball, but not in a medal round when you've a good score going.

For fairway bunkers of any depth think of two things: getting out of the bunker and *position*. Aim your recovery shot to where you will have a good flat lie and the best possible line to the green for

Left: **For a long bunker shot, you must have a solid stance, but don't go too deeply into the sand as this can produce a heavy shot.**

Right: **Always consider the position for your next shot.**

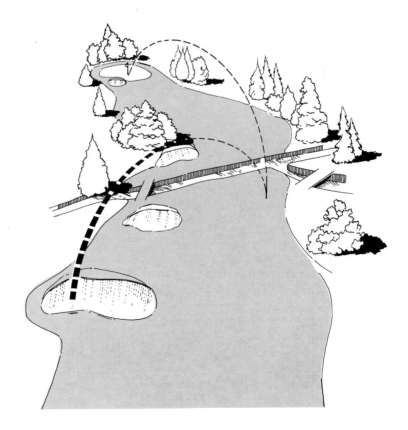

your next shot. Having an aim in mind will also help you to have a more definite attitude to the shot. You should be concentrating on the placement of your shot and not thinking that all you have to do is knock your ball out.

AROUND THE GREEN

The majority of bunkers designed to punish wayward shots into the green are just off, or even cut into, the putting surface. But there are others intended to catch balls which have fallen well short of the target, in the thirty to fifty yard range.

The long bunker shot

For shots from the bunkers in that thirty to fifty yard range, usually, the sand iron is the club to use. However, as you will often be trying to nip the ball cleanly from the sand, you will need to rely

less on its raised trailing flange. Your wedge or 9 iron may prove easier clubs to use as you will have to swing less hard with them. From a clean lie, play very much a short pitch shot but with your clubhead path parallel with the sand rather than descending towards it.

If you choose to stay with your sand iron, keep to your normal open stance for bunker shots but strike much nearer to the ball. A rule-of-thumb distance is about half an inch. How far your ball will travel should then be varied solely by the pace of your swing. Here, I can offer no guidance at all. It really is entirely a matter of feel, practice and playing experience. Even so, it is one of the shots that even tournament professionals of the highest class feel uneasy about, mainly because the difference between producing a successful shot and one that falls short or flies over the green is very slight.

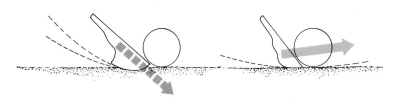

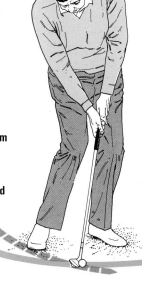

From a buried lie

When your ball descends almost vertically into a bunker, you may well have a ball half-buried.

There are many different ways of escaping. The most favoured one is to play the ball from mid-stance, square up the face of your sand wedge, make contact with the sand about two inches behind the ball, and keep the clubhead driving through. The ball will come out low, so this shot will not work if you're confronted by a steep bunker face. There will also be little, if indeed any, backspin so your ball will run much further than

Above: Sand iron *left* and wedge.

Right: Nipping the ball from hard sand for a long shot.

Below: Playing from a buried lie needs power and precision.

with a conventional bunker shot.

A variant of this is to keep your clubface a little open rather than square; otherwise use the same methods. At impact it is sometimes difficult to keep the clubface square. With either of these techniques, the real aim is to force sand at the ball, thus exploding it out. The closed face will tend to become square but, even so, the mass of your blade will be squarely driving the sand at the ball.

A third method was taught me by Chi Chi Rodriguez, that superb Puerto Rican. He believed that you should alter your normal bunker shot very little. Still play with an open blade, still make hard contact about two inches behind the ball and merely swing into it much faster. Imagine your clubhead going down, down, down. This is a rather more dangerous shot to attempt as you may not even get out but it does result in a slightly higher flight so that the ball will stop more quickly.

The disadvantage is that your more violent swing into the ball is more likely to contact the sand too near or too far away from it.

Again, experiment. See which of these

Above: **Closing the face of the sand wedge, with the hands forward.**

Right above: **Forcing the sand at and through the ball.**

Right below: **Imagine your clubhead is going well down, much further than it does.**

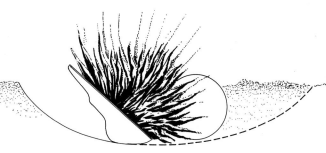

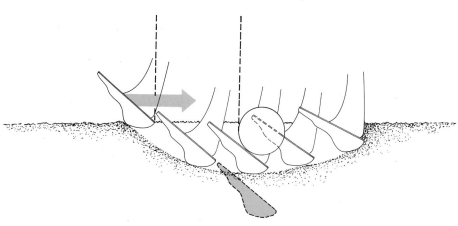

Hitting the ball from an
uphill buried lie.

methods suits you best and gives you confidence. My bet is that the square-face method is the easiest to manage, mainly because you don't have to swing hard at the ball and you should be able to prevent the blade from opening. For myself, I prefer Chi Chi's way. A compromise is to play with the square face when you have plenty of green to work with and the Rodriguez open-faced attack at other times.

Always remember that ball and clubhead will never be in contact. You are forcing the ball out with sand. Remember, too, that it's impossible to achieve much height with any of these methods if the ball is well down in the sand. There is no point at all if you're in a pot bunker to attempt the impossible. Look around you and decide on the most sensible escape route, which may well turn out to be sideways or even backwards. Settle for the loss of just one stroke.

The above applies to playing roughly from the middle of a bunker. But, what to do if your buried ball is well down at the rear in a downhill lie? If the bunker has any kind of face at all, it'll be impossible to go in that direction. Again, sideways or backwards is your only hope.

If the lie is uphill, even quite close to the face, you definitely have an easier problem to solve. Although your ball is still buried, there will be much less sand immediately behind it, and you can play your normal bunker shot. Do, however, try to visualize ball, sand and clubhead before you go into your swing. You must adjust your impact point according to the steepness of slope, contacting the sand further away from the ball.

The downhill lie

Almost always, downhill lies are found to the rear of bunkers. The most famous shot of this kind I've ever seen was performed – perhaps perpetrated would be a better word – by Lee Trevino at the 16th hole at Muirfield during the third round of the 1972 Open Championship. Lee, in an awkward spot, hit too near the ball. The result ought to have been another bunker shot from the other side of the green. But the gods were with him and he was lucky enough to hit the flagstick and down the ball dived for a birdie 2, part of a remarkable birdie sequence with which he completed a third round of 66.

Perhaps Trevino also played with rather too open a blade. If you do that, the danger with the downhill bunker lie is that you will skid over the sand rather than cut down into it. The result is either a shot hit too clean or simply topped.

Instead, move the ball further back in your stance, so that the leading edge of your club takes sand first, and just close the blade a little. Unless you are in a deep pot bunker, you'll still get sufficient height on the shot to get clear, but do remember to keep the clubhead moving forwards.

The uphill lie

Here we are back much more to a normal bunker shot. The only real difference in technique is that you should swing through the ball rather faster, unless you have a very short distance to go because the ball will come out on a high trajectory. Beware of taking sand too far behind the ball because with this kind of lie you are meeting a much greater weight of the stuff. Your club may dig in too far and you'll then fail to move the ball forwards and out.

Above: For an uphill lie drive into and through the sand, but be careful not to take too much.

Difficult stances

The American amateur Bob Lewis played a remarkable shot in the 1983 Walker Cup at Hoylake. He was bunkered left of the 16th green and very much towards the left-hand edge. His problem was how to stand to the ball. He tried this stance and that, attempting to get himself balanced enough to make at least a swing at the ball. He ended up on his knees and lo and behold, he came within a whisker of holing out! But that was luck as

Left: Playing from a downhill lie.

Right: Tom Watson playing a classic uphill bunker explosion shot.

well as improvisational genius.

Balance, indeed, is the problem. You have to forget all about your normal poised swing for a standard bunker shot and try to invent some way of standing to the ball so that you can still swing the club back and are balanced enough to bring the club back into the hitting area while still reasonably poised.

With a very difficult stance you can hardly hope for a perfect result. The aim is simply to get out or, at worst, move the ball along to a better lie. When, however, things are rather less extreme, keep the knees well flexed and also try to visualize the path and pace of the swing you're going to make. Rehearse it in your practice swing, even mentally if no practice swing is possible.

Plugged in the face.

Plugged in the face

Here again, some imagination is called for. Visualize how your clubhead will enter the sand (or of course it may well be mud) and the path it will then travel. Basically, though, getting out may not be quite as difficult as first thoughts would suggest. What you'll probably need to be trying to do is develop quite high clubhead speed, get in behind the ball at the right level and let the clubhead impacting into the sand or mud pop your ball out.

Under the bunker face

When you are under the bunker face quick height is needed. Play the ball from the normal bunker shot position – opposite the left foot – and have the clubface laid well back. Take the club back very steeply on the backswing and have the mental picture of coming equally steeply back to the ball. You need a U-shaped path of up- and downswing as a flatter arc gives less height to the ball.

How to get backspin

When you see a ball almost fizzing back from the turf, usually on the second bounce from a bunker shot, this may be the result of a number of factors, either separate or in combination:

1 You have probably seen it many times on TV. The greens will have received extra special preparation. The top surface may be a little on the soft side, which helps the ball to grip. The green may be tilting usefully. The grass may also be at its dense peak of perfection, rather like a really good Wilton carpet.

2 High flight on the ball, and a soft landing as a result, also maximize backspin.

3 Many golfers play all their shots from sand as an explosion. The clubhead enters the sand fairly well behind the ball and the forward movement of the sand takes the ball along with it. This creates backspin. It is the basic method of such masters of bunker play as the Americans Doug Ford, Julius Boros and Tom Watson, though I must stress that the amount of backspin does depend a great deal on the type of sand and the lie of the ball. Such players as these do not thump the clubhead into

the sand behind the ball; instead, they employ a slicing action, taking a shallow divot. The path of the clubhead is similar to the outline of a saucer, not a deep soup bowl. It enters the sand perhaps an inch or even less behind the ball and slides underneath. Because the clubface has cut across the line of flight, the ball lands with slice spin as well as backspin so the player should aim off to allow for the ball running sideways on landing.

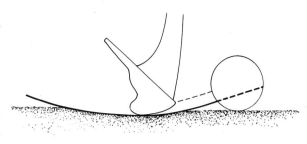

Wet sand

Wet sand also means hard sand, packed down by the weight of water.

From this kind of 'sitting up' lie, so many players just reach automatically for their sand iron. 'After all', they must reason, 'it's still a bunker shot, isn't it?'

My answer is, 'No, it isn't really.' What you should be attempting is something much nearer a short pitch shot. This is why.

A good bunker club should have a trailing edge quite a bit higher than the leading edge. Try to see, in your mind's eye, just what is all too likely to happen when you set up with the ball level with your front foot. That nicely rounded flange, designed to float through soft, fluffy sand, *bounces* from wet sand. The result is a thinned bunker shot

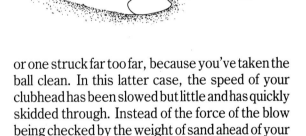

or one struck far too far, because you've taken the ball clean. In this latter case, the speed of your clubhead has been slowed but little and has quickly skidded through. Instead of the force of the blow being checked by the weight of sand ahead of your clubhead, and a shot of just a few yards resulting,

Above: 'Saucer' and 'soupbowl' clubhead paths.

Left: Getting backspin and slice spin.

you may well have produced something that is much nearer a full sand wedge approach from a fairway lie.

Instead, I suggest you regard this kind of bunker shot as a light, gentle pitch, using a wedge or 9 iron. For gaining confidence with it, there is no alternative to practice. It is more difficult to play than the same kind of shot from a comfortable fairway lie because the results of striking just a touch heavy or thin are rather more dire. In the first case, your club will cut quickly into the sand and the shot will be killed. In the second, you may well not clear any bunker face and if you do your ball will fly much further than intended.

If there is neither face nor lip on the particular bunker, why not think of using your putter. This may be a dangerous club to attempt from soft sand because it's very difficult to gauge the run of the ball. Much less so on wet sand, where your ball will run over the top, not through it.

However, you will have to try to predict how it will run over the undulations that will almost certainly exist. Your ball may also check or jump at the far edge of the bunker.

Make up your mind about the weight of stroke needed and then *don't change your mind* in midswing. The reason many putted shots from bunkers either die away before they've escaped from the sand, or alternatively pass the hole at high speed, is that the player hasn't really trusted his judgment.

Alas, I've even seen an air shot played. The man, as his putter head approached the ball, suddenly felt: 'My God, I'm not giving it enough.' And then tried to add a bit of pace with a convulsive heave of the body. Up and over the clubhead went. A sorry sight indeed and enough to make one stick to a more conventional shot.

A bare lie
Bare lies are much more often found on inland courses, especially if bunkers are not well maintained. The top covering, perhaps, has blown away, leaving the rather compacted soil beneath. Again, it isn't wise to play your sand iron. Use the

same approach as for a shot from wet sand, and look on it as a pitch shot.

Experience
Unless you play on a variety of courses, you are unlikely to become a good bunker player, though you may be effective enough on your own course. Your sand play will lack experience of playing from different kinds of sand. Here Gary Player was, indeed still is, supreme, as his performances in the 1984 US PGA showed. As the most international golfer of them all, he has seen just about everything. Locked away in his memory yet ready to be drawn on are experiences of playing from all kinds of lies in soft links sand, silica, grit, and even hard-baked clay. Of course, you can hardly hope for so much experience, but you can observe and learn every time you play a new course.

THE STANDARD BUNKER SHOT
It may seem a little eccentric of me to leave the first to last. However, I've been paying you the compliment of assuming that you can all make the basic shot. However, I do think it may be interesting to conclude bunker technique with a short revision course, especially as there isn't *one* correct way to play the shot.

I wonder if you remember the 1973 final of what was then called the Piccadilly World Matchplay Championship. It was between Australian Graham Marsh and Gary Player, reckoned to be the finest bunker player of all. The match finished on the 40th hole in a Player victory that seemed very much due to his mastery from sand. Marsh, as hole succeeded hole, had the upper hand through the green but Player survived by means of a bunker shot followed by a single putt. Perhaps those single putts are a fair part of the reason for Gary's reputation as so fine a sand player. It's little good consistently splashing the ball out to four or six feet if you then miss every putt. You may sometimes have seen those US Tour statistics and remember the category that ranks those with

the best success rate at getting down in two from greenside bunkers. Nearly always, the man heading the field is a superb putter.

Player's technique for the standard splash shot is rather different from the norm. He gets his weight well onto the front foot and his hands ahead of the ball, and then punches firmly into the sand behind the ball. When the lie is clean he varies only the pace of his swing and the distance his clubhead enters the sand behind the ball. For increased distance, he comes nearer to the ball and increases the pace of swing.

The Gary Player open-faced technique. You can almost feel the clubhead sliding under the ball, from three or four inches behind.

Most of the other great bunker players, including those just mentioned, have a very different approach to the art. They basically think in terms of sliding the clubhead under the ball, taking a sand divot some six to ten inches long. From fine links sand, they'll probably enter the sand, say three inches behind the ball and take a shallow divot – around the one inch mark. From coarse sand they strike about an inch nearer the ball and the divot will be at the two inch level. From wet sand, it's back to the shallow divot and the club will contact the sand about two inches behind the ball.

However, I don't want you to set about your bunker play with an imaginary tape measure in hand. The way to become knowledgeable and confident at bunker play is to practise. It is not at all easy to become a maestro and get everything stone dead (none of the experts do, as I've just said) but if you really know what you are doing you can make that delightful transition to *not* needing to worry about simply getting out but instead be easing the ball towards the flagstick.

Yet in my twenty years and more as a club professional I could just about count on the fingers of my hands the number of members I saw practising bunker shots. 'Why not?' I used to wonder, indeed still do. After all, if your living doesn't depend on it, practising putting is only truly exciting if suddenly they all start dropping infallibly and on the instant you 'know' you've found the magic formula. Few find their particular formula and it doesn't last. But nevertheless you'll usually see plenty of players having more than a few putts before they go for a round.

Bunker practice doesn't involve long walks and surely beats putting for interest. Perhaps you've never tried it. Believe me, it really is worth while to be able to know how to play the normal splash shot because you've done it successfully really quite often.

Alas, few clubs have a practice bunker, though I've been heartened in recent times to note that they are being seen more often. If yours is one of the clubs that still doesn't have one, make a nuisance of yourself. Write to the committee. If that doesn't work, buy the secretary or captain or chairman of the greens committee a drink, manoeuvre him into a corner and broach the subject again. Administer the dose again – and again – until it has an effect, or you end up singing!

Until then, you may feel it's worth while seizing the odd opportunity to have a couple or so practice shots from on course bunkers. Every little helps, you know.

You use your ordinary grip for the standard bunker shot. The other essentials are to set the ball well forward, about opposite the front instep, swing back steeply so that you get an out-to-in clubhead path and open the face of the club to the

target. Vary the length by whichever suits you best (perhaps a combination) of the following factors, all of which make the ball travel further:

1 More clubhead speed.
2 Less open face.
3 Clubhead enters sand nearer ball.
4 Shallower cuts through the sand.

Finally, watch good players. Providing the man has a reasonably even stance you should be able to feel the slow rhythm and tempo of the shot. It never appears to require any force at all. Back the clubhead slowly goes and then freewheels quite gently through sand and ball to a good follow-through.

The standard bunker shot.

CHOOSING A SAND IRON

Many club golfers don't 'choose' a sand iron at all; they buy a new set of irons and that's that. However, there are a few clubs which are highly individual: the driver, putter, perhaps a fairway wood, the wedge – and the sand iron. No golfer ever thinks of discarding his favourite putter just because he's equipping himself with a gleaming set of clubs, so likewise, if you've a sand iron that suits your touch and feel and is also suited to the bunker sand on your home course value it highly. Of course, I can't tell you anything about touch and feel – that's up to you. However, as regards the club design, I do have some very clear-cut and simple guidance.

All reasonably designed sand irons incorporate

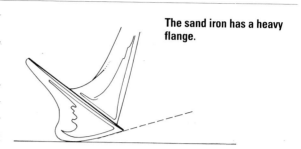

The sand iron has a heavy flange.

a heavy flange, slightly rounded, which forms the sole of the club. It has a leading and trailing edge, with the latter being higher. If you play most of your golf on a course or courses where the sand is both deep and light (fluffy, we often call it), usually found on links courses, you will most definitely need a club with more loft. This means, in more

Clubs with different angles of inversion are needed for different bunkers.

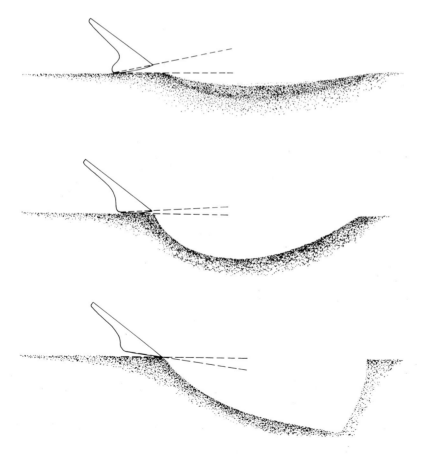

everyday terms, that the trailing edge is *much* higher than the leading one. The higher this edge, the less the club will dig down into the sand and the more it will ride through.

A club in which these characteristics are very pronounced may well be of little use to you for playing short pitches from the fairway, but you still have your wedge. The sight of the leading edge of the club well off the ground when you have taken up your stance and the lie is tight is not encouraging, and leads to negative thoughts. This edge does eventually become flush with the ground if you play the ball back in the stance but this lessens the loft of your club until it's much the same as your pitching wedge. You will probably then be best advised to use this type of sand iron just from bunkers and when you need the clubhead weight to play a hard, explosive shot from

To play a standard bunker shot, have the ball well forward and swing back steeply to get an out-to-in clubhead path.

deep rough, heather and gorse.

Few inland courses have the kind of sand I have been describing, unless they happen to have a very sandy subsoil. Most bunkering is basically artificial, with sand that has been distributed on what is often a clay subsoil. Here, you will want a sand iron where the trailing edge is only a little higher than the leading. The club that is highly suitable for links golf will strike the hard soil underlying the sand of these bunkers and bounce. The ball might then fly far over the green.

If you play golf on a considerable variety of courses two types of sand wedge can be useful.

When playing from a bunker on inland courses, be particularly observant about just where your ball is lying and the depth of the sand. In general, the sand is progressively deeper from the middle to the edges – everyone rakes bunker sand from the middle outwards. Also, the surface is much more compacted by the weight of many golfers in the middle because that is where the average trapped ball comes to rest. You may well profit from using your sand iron from lies towards the edges of a bunker but a wedge or 9 iron from the middle. Remember, you *are* allowed to 'test the surface' of a bunker by wriggling your feet and this should tell you what you need to know. If you can feel hard ground just below the sandy surface, don't play your sand iron.

Of course, this shouldn't really be so, given good bunker maintenance. In an ideal world, a bunker should be dug out twice a year at the very least. It just isn't good enough to shovel new sand on top of a compacted sub-surface. However,

while there are plenty of complaints about 'untidy' bunkers and how 'That fourball in front of us never once smoothed over their footprints,' you seldom hear a word raised about good maintenance of the subsoil of a bunker.

So, be aware of this particular problem and adjust your choice of club accordingly.

There is another type of sand wedge that is really a beast which tries to do two jobs and succeeds none too well at either. It was brought out a good many years ago and christened the 'dual purpose' sand wedge. It often has a heavy rounded sole but the leading and trailing edges of the flange are at an equal height. It is quite effective for pitching, even though the leading edge by no means sits flush with the turf, but it should not be used in bunkers with soft sand as it will not ride through the sand correctly and will only do an effective job in bunkers when the sand is comparatively shallow, and the subsoil rather firm.

If you feel that you play bunker shots well enough but the results are unsatisfactory this really might be an occasion when you may be justified in blaming your tools. Why not be sys-

Above: 'Dual purpose' sand wedge *left* and ordinary sand iron. *Below:* Most people rake bunkers from the middle.

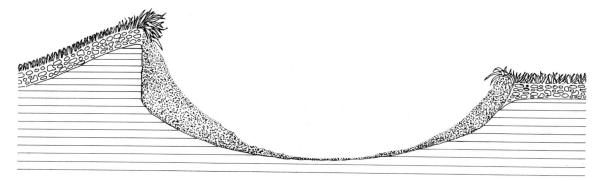

tematic about it and, one quiet summer's evening, borrow a range of sand irons from your golfing chums and then, bearing my general principles in mind, see which one you do best with? Many is the top professional who, early in his career, has been none too good from bunkers but has then discovered a sand iron which made precise sand play suddenly much easier.

As a young amateur, Bernard Gallacher confessed he was by no means a good bunker player, and when he turned professional he was soon aware how much higher the standards were. The former Ryder Cup captain, his fellow Scotsman Eric Brown, put young Bernard straight by telling him that he was using an unsuitable club. He lent him a good one and almost on the instant Gallacher's bunker play improved.

A really well designed sand iron does do half the job for you. A bad one can prevent you from making real progress in your bunker technique.

Bernard Gallacher playing a plugged bunker shot very close to the flag.

TROUBLESOME STANCES AND LIES

Whatever our golf course, I doubt if we play even half our shots through the green from a dead flat stance with the ball sitting exactly as we like it. It has a nasty habit of landing on slopes, in patches of rough, too close to trees, or in small depressions where it is not easy to get the clubhead at the ball. These situations call for a change in either our mental approach or in our playing technique – or most likely both.

DIVOTS AND CUPPED LIES

The problem with any tight lie is to get the full face of the clubhead into the back of the ball. The more the bottom of the ball lies below the surrounding surface, the more difficult the shot.

In a slightly cupped lie, it helps merely to 'sit down' a touch more than usual. This makes your clubhead arc in the hitting area just that fraction of an inch lower. If you need distance on the shot, remember that the small head and fairly rounded sole of a fairway wood will fit the shape of the ground far better than the longer and flatter sole of a long iron. For this kind of shot, resist the temptation to lift the club up sharply and to hit down on the ball. Reserve this for more difficult lies. Just make your normal swing, striving for a

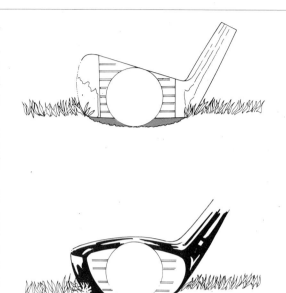

Iron *top* and fairway wood.

It is difficult to get the club on to a ball sitting down in a partly grown-in divot.

precise hit and maintaining good balance through the ball. It will certainly help to achieve both of these aims if you concentrate on swinging smoothly rather than flat out. Make sure your swing pattern is the same.

This procedure applies equally well when your ball has come to rest in a shallow or partly grown-in divot.

One way of playing from a divot is to slide the clubhead across and under the ball. However, this is always a risky shot, and there's no need to make the game more difficult than it already is. Most divots are found in the areas of fairway where players' drives come to rest, especially when there are slopes. On average, you could be playing to the green from a divot. How you decide to play the particular shot will have to be decided by what lies between you and the flag.

If there's no obstruction, I'd suggest the punch shot as the best. Play the ball a touch further back in your stance, set your weight 60 per cent on the front foot, and don't take a full swing. The three-quarter position is about right for you if you normally go back to the horizontal. Set up with your hands ahead of the ball, maintaining that relationship through impact. Hit down and through, keeping the wrists firm and the clubhead square to the line. Grip more firmly than usual with both hands. This will lessen the poorness of the shot if you are unfortunate enough to meet the ground a little before the ball. You will get a shot with backspin but lower flight than usual so the ball will run further. Make allowances for this.

If, however, there's a bunker between you and

Right: Sandy Lyle stamping balls into the ground in order to practise precise striking.

Below: Playing the punch shot.

the flag you can do one of two things. Your first alternative is to accept that you may well have to concede a shot to par and play short, or indeed to the side of the green if that'll give you a better chance of getting down in two more. You may, however, decide to go for the flag, in which case you will obviously need a shot as high as you'd expect from a normal lie. Play the ball from the normal position (just inside the front heel) but have the mental picture of a steeper backswing, breaking the wrists earlier, and a sharp downwards approach to the ball. As it's essential to be very firm indeed through the hitting area, it may help if you open the clubface a touch. You can then strike more decisively and get a higher flight. However, negative thoughts may wash into your mind. You have to conquer such thoughts. Keep your mind clear and be decisive. If you can't, put the club back in the bag and think of less risky alternative courses of action.

With either of these techniques, I advise you to avoid the sand iron unless you have bags of confidence in the club. That trailing edge may bounce and produce a thinned shot.

Confidence is very important. All a shot from a divot or cupped lie asks is that you strike precisely. I remember watching Sandy Lyle practising a few years ago. He was experiencing some trouble with his striking and wanted to make things more difficult for himself. He took out a wood and stamped the ball down so that it was half buried. Shot after shot flew away just as well as if his ball had been nicely set up on a tee peg. Yet he seemed to have no chance at all of getting the middle of the clubhead into the back of the ball. Precise striking, indeed.

FLUFFY LIES

At professional tournaments, a howl usually goes up if the fairways aren't closely shaven. Not so club golfers. Most love to see the ball sitting up and would like to hit it off something similar to a new scrubbing brush.

The tournament player, however, only likes that cushion of grass under his ball when playing a wood. For the irons, it's another story. He wants to squeeze his ball between clubhead and turf, as this gives him a far more predictable result and more backspin. In America, where there's a standard length of cut for both tournament greens and fairways, the fairways resemble a Wilton carpet with a tight, short pile. However, things are still far less sophisticated in Britain, where not one course is as well manicured as hundreds in the USA. American pro's are therefore less likely to have to contend with fluffy lies than the British. The flyer is to be feared.

This is a shot that comes 'hot' from the blade, goes further through the air than anticipated, and has relatively little backspin. It leaves you well through the green – perhaps out of bounds or in the members' dining room.

How then can techniques be altered to avoid

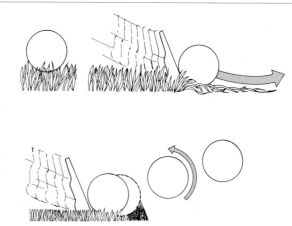

Above: **Squeezing the ball into the turf gets more backspin.**

Right: **Seve's flyer from the rough on the 17th at the Open, St Andrews 1984.**

this kind of shot?

Let's suppose the tournament player is some 130 yards from the green. From a normal lie he might hit a full wedge or perhaps a far more gentle shot with a 7 iron – it all depends how he thinks he will get the best result. For him, the worst situation from this distance is to find his ball sitting up in wet grass, perhaps in the semi-rough.

Negative thoughts flood in. He has various alternatives and doesn't really know if any of them will work. Shall I hit my full wedge and hope it doesn't fly? Shall I hit a sand iron and hope it does? Or perhaps try to run it with a rather gentle 7 iron, landing well short?

If he wants to be safe, and there are no bunkers between him and the flag, the last alternative is the one to follow, as he won't be hitting hard enough for the ball to fly really destructively.

If there are bunkers in his way, then he must think tactically. Perhaps he should stay with that 7 iron and play short, leaving himself with an open shot to the flag for the next shot. If there's no real trouble through the green, he would go for a shot with the wedge.

Of course, you may never have had a flyer in your life. I hardly had one myself but professionals these days are very fond of claiming that any

approach they send well through was a flyer. Perhaps they are more likely to suffer them as they tend to hit approach shots harder than I used to like.

But if you do hit flyers, take heart – the one shot that did the most to win Ballesteros the 1984 championship at St Andrews was a flyer. Playing the 17th in the last round, Seve was in the left rough. He decided he had a flying lie. He lashed a 6 iron and it did fly, finishing on the green in a good position for the putt. Tom Watson, from a perfect lie in the ideal fairway position, was playing a 2 iron. There is that much difference between a normal lie and a flying one.

BARE LIES (HARD PANS)

Bare lies (hard pans) are not really troublesome at all for long shots, and shouldn't worry the good striker, provided the ground is firm. Indeed, good players actually prefer a hard bare lie, as there is no grass between clubface and ball to prevent crisp contact. Even a driver can be played from such a lie if you think in terms of sweeping the ball away, concentrating on the middle, not the bottom, of the ball.

Even ordinary strikers can get good distance with this shot. Aim to make contact with the top half of the ball. If you don't strike it perfectly, it will still bound and skip a long way in dry summer conditions.

Where the bare lie can create difficulties is in short pitches. Almost all the top professionals like to reach for a sand iron when they're close to the green and the lie is good. They feel that they can calculate exactly where they want the ball to pitch and not have to worry about any great length of run. But when the lie is bare, they fear that the big heavy flange may catch the ground just before impact with the ball, with the bounce of the clubhead producing a thinned shot. Alternatively there is a possibility that the ball may be met low on the clubhead, resulting in far more run than was wanted.

When this is the case, it's still possible to play

the ball further back in your stance, from a position where you are confident that the rear of the flange won't get you into trouble. Perhaps pause for thought then. You've 'delofted' your sand iron and might just as well play a normal wedge shot.

The great modern exponents of the shot include Tom Watson, Seve Ballesteros, Bernhard Langer and the older maestro, Neil Coles. Notice their secret. All swing the clubhead back surprisingly far and control the speed of the swing, ensuring that the clubhead is still accelerating as it meets the ball, however slowly they appear to swing.

Another way of playing these little shots from bare lies is to move the ball back very little in your stance, set your weight sixty/forty towards the front foot and break the wrists early. This will give you a more upright swing plane and enable you to drop the clubhead on the ball. That's the Gary Player method. This is a shot you can perfect even in the back garden, for little space is needed. See whether the sand iron or another pitching club suits you best.

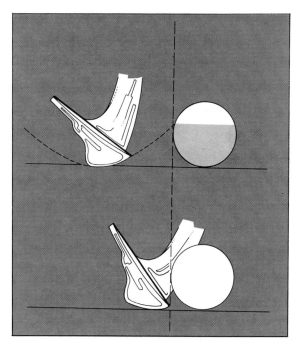

UPSLOPES AND DOWNSLOPES

If you make no adjustments at all, you are likely to hit the turf then the ball when going uphill and thin or half-top from a sloping lie. So let's think about the basics.

On upslopes the ground sets your weight back towards your rear foot. Compensate for this by consciously getting a little more weight on your front foot. Make sure that you swing back particularly easily to avoid a sudden and jerky weight transfer to your back foot. It'll help if you think in terms of hands and arms rather than a big body turn. Balance is all important – together with sensible club selection.

As regards choice of club, try to visualize (it's not too difficult) what the *real* loft of the club will be as it strikes the ball. If there's a severe upslope, you might well think of using as much as three more clubs than from a flat lie. That's how much the angle of clubface to ball can be changed. An alternative, though not one that I favour, is to play the ball further back in your stance. This reduces the extra clubhead loft caused by playing from an uphill lie.

My basic thought, however, is that shots from gentle upslopes are easy – even for below-average golfers. The back, even the bottom of the

Left: **The rear flange can hit the ground before the club hits the ball.**

Right: **The Gary Player method for playing from bare lies, dropping the clubface on the ball.**

ball, looks very inviting. It's almost like hitting from a tee peg. The only difficulty is that of maintaining balance, and that's best achieved by swinging smoothly, back and through with hands and arms working as a one. The harder you swing, the more you're likely to topple over, and a good shot becomes a matter of sheer luck.

Downslopes are, however, more difficult for golfers at all levels. There's a far greater chance of

Right: An inviting ball.

Above: On an upslope adjust the line of your shoulders and body so as to feel comfortable.

Below: For either up or downslopes align yourself so that a perpendicular line through your body would meet the ground at a right angle.

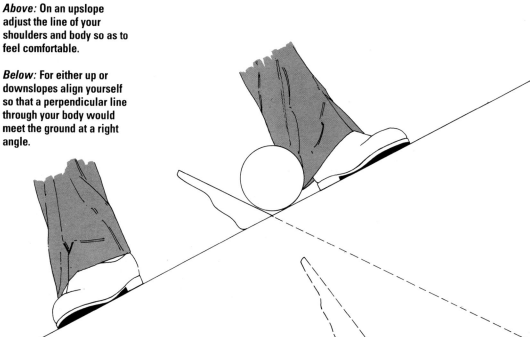

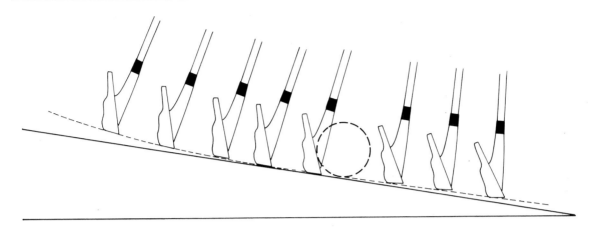

either thinning your shot or hitting turf before ball. And that ball, I must emphasize, is never going to look as if it's nicely teed up ready for you to hit it.

Still set your weight towards the front foot and maintain it there right through impact. There'll be a tendency to lift up; obviously this must be resisted. Have the mental image of your clubhead keeping on the target line through and beyond the ball. Above all, stay down on the shot. Use a more lofted club because you'll automatically hood the face – the reverse of playing uphill. Again, don't hit too hard. Even the greatest stars can make this mistake. Don't try to nip or pluck the ball off the surface but do keep your club down, following the line of the slope.

With both up- and downslopes, try to align yourself so that a perpendicular line through your body meets the shape of the ground as near a right angle as is comfortable. If you do this, you'll be adjusting your swing path so that the effect of either up- or downslope is naturally lessened. Even so, this is only possible on fairly gentle slopes. Otherwise, the key with both shots is to maintain rhythm and balance and be bold in varying your choice of club when slopes are severe. Always analyse the problem before taking any action and ensure that you feel happy with your decision so you can carry through your solution with confidence.

Above: **Keep the clubface following the contours of the ground as much as possible.**

Below: **Playing on a downslope – play down on the shot.**

SIDESLOPES

Sideslopes always produce balance problems. The less well balanced the basic swing and the more severe the slope, the greater the difficulties.

As every golfer knows, the ball below the feet is a far greater problem than the ball above the feet, so I'll give this situation correspondingly more attention.

If you've a distinctly flat swing and the slope is steep, you've very little chance of playing even a remotely passable shot unless you make adjustments, some of which will feel unnatural.

Basically, the ball is too far away, isn't it? How do we attempt the impossible of bringing it nearer? It can be done – in a way:

1 Grip the club at the very end of the shaft.
2 'Sit down' to the ball more than usual, with plenty of 'give' in the knees.

Ball below the feet.

3 If you've a flat swing, tilt forwards from the hips. Don't, however, let this movement become one of bending the back. The tilt will compel your swing to be more upright.
4 Move closer to the ball.

These changes will largely conquer the problem of ball distance. We're left with balance and the tendency to slice.

Good balance and swinging a golf club just don't mix when on a severe slope – after all, we aren't mountain goats. But, unless your home course is very hilly, you don't have to deal with these often. When you do come across them, make sure you don't get your weight too much on the toes and balls of your feet but don't go to the other extreme, setting it all on the heels. Around the heel side of the balls of your feet is the best compromise. Feel the slope and rehearse your shot. Let your body flow with the shape of the ground. You'll find that your shoulder turn will be restricted if you're to maintain reasonable balance in the hitting area (this is one occasion when a good finish to your swing is unlikely).

If you are slicing in this situation, it will probably be for one of two reasons. Firstly, as you push the clubhead further away from you, the face may be falling open. Secondly, your restricted shoulder turn means that you are much more likely to hit from outside to in. For the first of these set the clubface more shut. It will then still be more or less square when you actually ground it behind the ball. For the second you will probably find it helpful to play the ball from a little further back in your stance – near the middle rather than inside the front heel.

Many shots in golf are a compromise and this is certainly a time when you shouldn't attempt too much. As you've got to maintain the best control and balance you can, don't blaze away with a wood or long iron. Choose a club that's shorter in the shaft and therefore easier to control. Be content to play for position.

Finally, if a little experimentation has proved that you'll still slice, the answer to that one is quite simple. Why not allow for it? Most of the greats do

Left: Hitting a ball below the feet on a sideslope often produces a slice. If you find you cannot correct this, then allow for it.

Below: Positioning for a ball above the feet.

just that, so you can do the same.

The position with the ball above the feet, provided that the slope is gentle, is relished by many golfers at club level. Because we have more of a sight of the ball than from a normal flat lie, it looks a very inviting target. In particular, the flat swinger can sweep it away with relish.

In almost every instance we reverse the process from the ball below the feet. Here are the definite 'dos':

1 Shorten the grip for accuracy if length is not required.

2 Make sure your spine is erect, which makes for a flatter swing arc.

3 Stand tall, that is, restrict any tendency to 'sit down' to the shot.

4 Note that because the ball is nearer, your clubface may become a little shut. Either open it or simply aim off, perhaps ten yards.

5 Prevent your weight falling too much on your heels.

6 Swing easily, even gently. You'll still get lots of distance.

LOW SHOTS

The most usual cause of low shots is trees – often when a wild hit has been made from the tee 'into the woods'. It's also not at all unusual to find what would normally be a simple high pitch to the green impeded by an overhanging branch, or perhaps a course has a tree 'unfairly' set in mid-fairway so that what ought to be a simple second shot has to be kept low.

The first essential is to get off to the right start by selecting a sensible club. Confronted with an approach shot of seventy to 100 yards under an obstacle, where they'd normally have reached for a wedge, many golfers don't make the right choice. They start by going for a club with less loft, but aren't drastic enough, and settle, perhaps, for a 7 or 8 iron.

What happens? Well, the ball does fly lower but not low enough and there's a tell-tale clatter.

How much more sensible to select a club where you feel it'd be impossible for you to get the ball up high enough, even if you tried! Think 5 iron, going down the shaft to increase your control over the clubhead.

The reason why golfers will not often consider a longer iron is that they are used to playing gentle shots only with short irons. They are also afraid they'll fizz the ball through the green or, alternatively, dribble it along the ground well short. In fact, the answer lies in trying the shot in practice – nothing too strenuous. Just a dozen or so strokes will increase confidence no end, and show that you can quite easily control the shot.

It helps to make changes in both ball and hand position. Move the ball back to mid-stance and have the mental picture of your hands being ahead of the clubhead at impact. You may find it easier to achieve this if you widen your stance, for this will automatically bring your hands further ahead of the ball. Keep the clubhead square with the target line. Don't hood or open the face unless you need a slice or hook shape to your shot.

Keep the wrists firm throughout with everything in that area feeling solid. It's easy enough to hit quite a high shot even with a 3 iron if you end up by giving the ball a wristy flick. You can then let the clubhead get well in front of the hands. If you do this, you very much increase the loft of the face. Also, you'll open it up.

Make sure that you're pulling the clubhead through the ball. The whole feel of the shot should not be greatly different from playing a long putt or

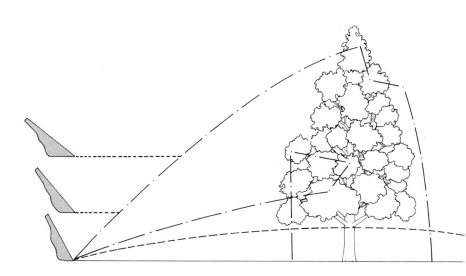

Think about the angle of loft on your club when having to hit under an obstacle.

Hitting under an obstacle.

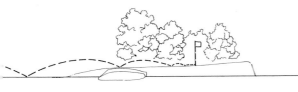

chip. Swing slowly; keep the hand action easy and the wrists dead.

. Very much the same applies to playing a *long* second shot under an obstacle. However, as you are now making a full swing this will have much more backspin, causing the ball to rise quickly. It is even more important, then, to use a club with little loft. You just have to accept that you aren't likely to play a perfect shot. This could be a time when a driver hit a little thin, skipping along the ground, could be a very good shot indeed. Go down the shaft a little to increase control. Indeed, follow all the advice above for playing far shorter shots.

HIGH SHOTS

If you want to hit *over* an obstacle, the remarks above about the choice of club for hitting under one also apply, but otherwise the procedure is the opposite. The essentials are:

1 Ball forward of its normal position in your stance.

2 Hands should not be ahead of the clubhead.

3 Grip at the top of the shaft.

4 Narrow your stance a touch. This will help you not to contact the ground before you reach the ball.

5 Strive for a lively feel in the hands and wrists, which will help get the clubhead moving both through and *under* the ball.

6 Hit full out. The extra backspin on any full shot means inevitably, whatever the club you're using, that your ball will rise more abruptly.

Hitting over an obstacle.

Finally one don't. It's death to try to help your ball up into the air. Let the club do the work. Still hit down and through.

As with any specialized shot, it's always as well to build up your experience and confidence. I don't suggest you should go out and see if you can knock them over the clubhouse roof at point-blank range in front of the secretary's office. Instead, find a bush. See how near you can get to it and still fly the ball over. For longer shots, a tree is the obvious choice. I guarantee you'll be amazed at how high it's possible to hit with a club such as a 6 iron.

But don't be 'carried away' in competitive play. Choose a club you're sure will get you over and accept loss of distance.

IN THE ROUGH

This short phrase encompasses a vast variety of situations. At the one extreme you can be nicely sitting up in a lie good enough to take a driver, and at the other the sensible course might be to take the medicine of a one-stroke penalty for an unplayable lie.

So let's go through the card, going from bad, to better, to ideal.

The unplayable lie doesn't at all mean what the words seem to say. For the individual golfer, it may well be a matter of deciding that either you cannot move your ball or that you will only succeed in moving it to just as unsatisfactory a place. One classic example of this was Tom Weiskopf in the 1973 British Open at Troon. From the 9th tee in his third round the drive finished well down in the gorse. I dare say he had a fifty-fifty chance of getting it back to the fairway but Tom decided the risk was not worth taking. He deemed his ball unplayable and walked back about a hundred yards until he found a patch of more promising ground. He had decided that, for him, the chance of a successful recovery to the fairway was not worth the risk. Also, by going back so far, he made full and legitimate use of the Rules of Golf. He didn't just pick his ball out from an evil place and play from somewhere little better. Tom was prepared to sacrifice all that distance for the prospect of a good lie. He took 6, true enough, on a par 4 – but he went on to win the championship. More recently, playing the 542 yard 15th at Royal Birkdale, a par 5, in the 1983 championship, Tom Watson pushed his second shot away to the right into dense willow scrub. In this case, his ball was truly unplayable. There-after, like Weiskopf, he walked back until he found an area likely to give him a good enough lie. Again, the result was a 6. Again the player concerned finished as Open Champion.

I don't mean to suggest that these decisions won the championship for either Weiskopf or Watson. But they did avoid *losing* it by making a sensible decision, and kept in control.

When in this position your thought processes should go something like this:

1 Can I manage to bring the clubhead into contact with the ball?

2 Can I be reasonably sure of not just moving it along to another horrid place?

Unless the answer to both of these questions is 'Yes', be sane and sensible and deem your ball unplayable. Don't just think that there's a sporting chance that you might manage what you have in mind.

When you are well down amongst the grass roots or well obstructed by heather, broom or gorse, not too far from the fairway or green, the sand iron is the club to use. Its extra clubhead weight is useful and you can play something similar to a bunker shot, hitting the ball a couple of inches behind, assuring you of the high flight needed to escape from long grass or whatever ails you.

With a poor lie where the path of the clubhead into the ball is obstructed, start thinking about what your clubhead is going to meet, and the flight of the ball after a reasonably successful contact. I am not one of those who winces in horror at the sight of a handicap golfer reaching for a wood. Indeed, something of the order of a 7 wood with a small head can be the best club of all to use in the range between poor and good lies off the fairway.

A sharp angle of loft is needed to get out of long grass.

Your 3 or 4 wood can come into use once the lie is a fairly clean one. What you really should not con-sider, unless the ball is sitting up nicely, are the long irons. If you are tempted, recall the sad fate of Arnold Palmer in 1966. He threw away the US Open *twice* in Billy Casper's direction (losing a vast lead in both the final round and the 18 hole play-off). In both championships the main cause of his downfall was the same. Trusting in his formid-able hand and forearm power, he asked his caddie for long irons when pitching clubs were the sensible choice. Though he made reasonable ball contact, his shots were choked by long grass before they were fully airborne.

Basically, then, I suggest that from anything

129

that isn't quite a good lie you think in terms of a lofted wood and, with the irons, nothing with less loft than a 6.

In good lies, however, you can be as daring as you like. For instance, club players seldom think of taking their driver though the ball may be perched up just as invitingly as if it were on a tee. But perhaps there's some wisdom in this. Merely the fact of the longer shaft makes a safe shot less likely. It is therefore probably best to reserve taking your driver for occasions when the possible extra length will give you some really worthwhile advantage.

Water, on the other hand, is very hard stuff indeed. Apart from the very doubtful chance of success, it's worth considering whether or not the risk of injury is really worth it. My own rule-of-thumb would be to attempt water shots only if the ball lies on a reasonably firm bottom with no more than half of it below the surface. As you probably haven't had much practice with the shot – it takes some dedication to get one's feet wet – I also suggest you attempt the shot only when playing towards near-by dry land. In other words, don't try to carry your ball from one side of a small pond to the other.

Because there are so many more water hazards on American courses, their stars can draw on their experience to produce surprisingly good shots. Some reckon to be able to recover from several inches deep but I'm not sure I believe them!

The basic method of playing the shot is similar to the bunker shot, though this time the splash is a very real one! Line up with the clubface square or slightly open, swing back fairly steeply and make contact about two inches behind the ball, driving down and forwards very firmly indeed. As with a bunker shot, don't roll the wrists, and maintain the square or open clubface to the finish. However, if you are in any doubt, take a penalty drop. It's very easy to go 'over the top' of the ball if it is totally submerged. Also, if you are attempting the near-impossible, do remember to wear your waterproofs.

RESTRICTED BACKSWINGS

In golf, most us spend much of our time trying to achieve a mechanical perfection in hitting a ball from a perfect lie with a perfect full swing. However, all the expertise we may have achieved is set at naught when we hit a wayward shot and find the next one has to be played with branch, bush, wall or whatever impeding our backswing.

In this situation, what all too many club golfers do is jerk the clubhead back for a very short distance indeed, probably well short of the obstacle, and heave it into the ball with all the body action they can muster. Result: zero – or worse.

Even if you recognize yourself in my description, I hope you'll admit that this is all wrong. As an Open Championship competitor I've played the Old Course at St Andrews in many Championships and seen lots of players hard up against the wall alongside the 17th green. A goodly number extricate themselves cleanly and efficiently. True, they seldom float or run the ball to within inches of the hole, but almost invariably they succeed, with a restricted backswing, in getting it on the green. Sometimes near enough to single putt.

Usually, even as quick a player as Tom Watson takes quite a long time over sizing up the shot. Others seem to take an age – but the waiting may be worth it. Whereas for all 'normal' shots, there is very little if anything gained by playing slowly, when you are improvising a backswing do give yourself time to get the feel of the shot. Rehearse it. Rehearse it a few more times. Then do what you've rehearsed. All too often, that 'doing it' is the disaster point. Always remember how far your ball will travel from a short backwing and quite gentle hit if your timing is right. Take the club back slowly and don't race back down.

I suggest that you rehearse a shorter backswing than actually needed to stay short of the obstacle to remove those nagging doubts about making contact with it. You can also give yourself more room by going down the grip and even on to the shaft. You may also find it useful to play the ball well back in your stance, even as far as the

When up against a tree, you may have to improvise.

rear foot and rely on a steep chop down at the ball. Make allowances, though, for the fact that you've made the loft of, say, a wedge into something like a 5 iron. But beware. Many of these shots fail through coming off the clubface too low and dying in the first few feet of rough.

Providing you've got a good lie, don't be afraid of using a fairly straightfaced iron (though not from too far back in your stance). You can get a surprising amount of distance with something not much more than a scuffle with a 3 iron instead of trying a more full swing with a pitching club.

If the impediment to your backswing is twigs and light branches, try out a full swing or two. You may find it's possible to swing through the obstruction. However, it takes very little resistance to sap the confidence. Also, don't forget the Rules of Golf. You're not allowed actually to break twigs and branches with your practice swings, thus improving your position. If you are up against a

truly solid obstruction – the bole of a tree or the foot of a fence post, for example – then think of changing hands, a right-hander playing a left-handed stroke. Use either a normal grip or reversed-hands if that feels more comfortable and use the toe of the club you select. This is well worth some practice in the garden. Also, there's nothing in the Rules of Golf that says you may not use the back of the club. Look at it and give thought to how the ball will behave. There's even the one-handed shot. Stand alongside the ball with your back to the target. Hold the club at the bottom of the grip. You should easily get 20 yards.

Finally it is always worth considering the putter when in out-of-the-way places. Many centre shafts are almost worth another club in the bag because the face is very much the same either side of the blade. The blade putter also has its uses, as its short shaft helps you to control the club when you swing from the wrong side.

If you are caught with a restricted backswing, try to swing through the ball. Don't just stab at it.

THE MENTAL GAME

When a player becomes a major championship winner, we naturally have a tendency to think it's all because he has a magnificent swing and the hand-to-eye coordination to produce exact striking. Yet this is only a part of the story. You may have a young assistant professional at your own club who seems to have all the talents yet in the fire of competition doesn't do at all well. There's very much more to golf than just being able to play the shots. Much of what goes on in this individual and sometimes lonely game is in the mind.

COURSE MANAGEMENT

Throughout his long dominance of championship golf, Jack Nicklaus was considered by many pundits not only to be the best player in the world, but perhaps the best ever.

Yet there's certainly doubt if he was definitely the best in any single department of the game. Yes, he certainly was an immense hitter in the 1960s – but a few were longer. Other players were a little shorter than Jack but more likely to keep the ball on the fairway. For placement of the tee shot, Nicklaus could not rank with Byron Nelson, Ben Hogan, Gene Littler or Don January. From sand, he was inferior to a host of players, so much so that Lee Trevino was moved to remark that his fellow professionals were fortunate that Jack was 'born without a sand iron'. Here Sam Snead, Gene Littler, Gary Player, Chi Chi Rodriguez, and indeed Trevino himself, were vastly superior players.

As late as the end of 1979, Nicklaus was conscious enough of other flaws in his game to take action on them. He sought help from short-game expert Phil Rodgers on chipping and on short pitching.

So we're left with putting and long iron play. Here again, there were better putters – Bob Charles, Billy Casper, Ben Crenshaw and Tom Watson for instance – but not many of them. And Jack had one vital ability: no one was better at getting the putts down in the four- to twelve-foot range when it really counted.

As a long iron player he was certainly superior. I think he's the best I've seen as a striker of the 1 and 2, helped by the fact that he played these clubs with a controlled swing and hardly ever as a flat-out hit.

So what's the verdict? Here is a player who was superb in only one or two departments, but, while good, was bettered in all the others. Yet he piled up major championship win after win, while technically not as complete a player as Seve Ballesteros or Tom Watson today would appear to be.

What gave Jack the edge?

Three things. He was certainly not bad at any department of the game. He had supreme nerve in a crisis. And he knew how to manage a golf course – what he called himself 'course management'. This is what it means.

Nicklaus never takes up a club, from the tee to the last putt, without thinking out what he's trying to achieve with each shot and the best way of doing it.

Take the driver, for instance. He generally uses it only when there is little trouble around the driving area or when he can't reach the green in regulation without it.

If length is not going to be a great advantage, Nicklaus then moves on to considering what is the

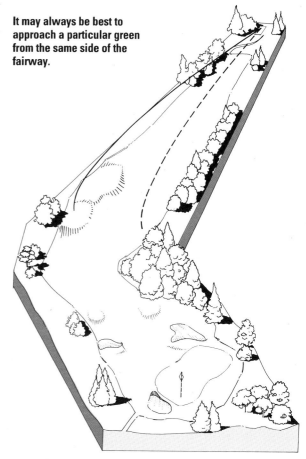

It may always be best to approach a particular green from the same side of the fairway.

best part of the fairway. After all, a drive just sets you up to play the rest of the hole.

This, then, is a key to improving your golf, and much can be learned from Nicklaus's approach. Many golfers at club level just want the thrill of 'getting a good one' away (preferably the longest in their fourball), but what they should be thinking about is which part of the fairway will give them the best approach to the green.

Several factors will be involved here:

1 It may *always* be best to approach the particular green from the left or right half of the fairway, whatever the wind or ground conditions. On the other side, you may be partially blocked out by trees or find the ground obstructed by bunkers or humps or hollows. There may be no bunkers and the ground might be flat on the side that you should chose.

2 Depending on the pin position on the particular day a shot to either left or right on holes that don't come into our first category will give you the best line in.

3 You should always be wanting to find a flat lie for your next shot. If a long drive will reach either an up or downslope, it's sensible to play short. A 5-iron, for example, played from a flat lie, is more likely to be successful than a 7 played from a severe slope.

4 Being close to the green for your second shot need not always be an advantage, say at a hole of little more than 300 yards. Many players are none too happy playing half or finessed shots that alight, as Trevino puts it, 'Like a butterfly with sore feet'. There is little point in hitting a drive to within fifty or sixty yards of the flag (which will require that kind of shot) if you feel more comfortable hitting a full sand wedge from around 100 yards. Think of the players at Augusta in the Masters. Usually, if they get into a water hazard in front of the green, they will walk a good many yards back so that they can hit a firmer shot with the greater backspin that results.

Once you are in a good position to play your shot to the green, it's time to think of what's the safest shot just to get you on the green and what part of the green offers the best chances of either a possible one-putt or at least being down in two. Here are some thoughts worth bearing in mind.

1 If there's a bunker between you and the flag, and little ground to work with on the green, think about how well you're hitting your irons on the day. If it's a wedge shot, ask yourself if you're capable of getting the exact length needed to get you *just* over the bunker, rather than in it. Can you keep negative thoughts in control? Remember also that there is very likely no point at all in taking a stronger club and hitting it well past the flag. Why not just play wide of the bunker in the first place, hoping to leave yourself a putt of ten yards or so?

2 Give thought to whether it's safer to be short than long, or vice versa. Are there bunkers,

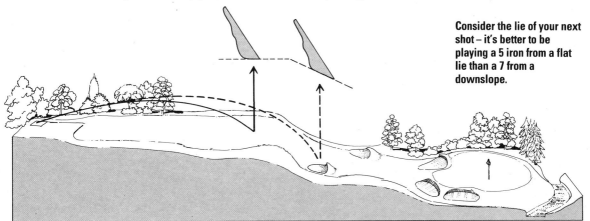

Consider the lie of your next shot – it's better to be playing a 5 iron from a flat lie than a 7 from a downslope.

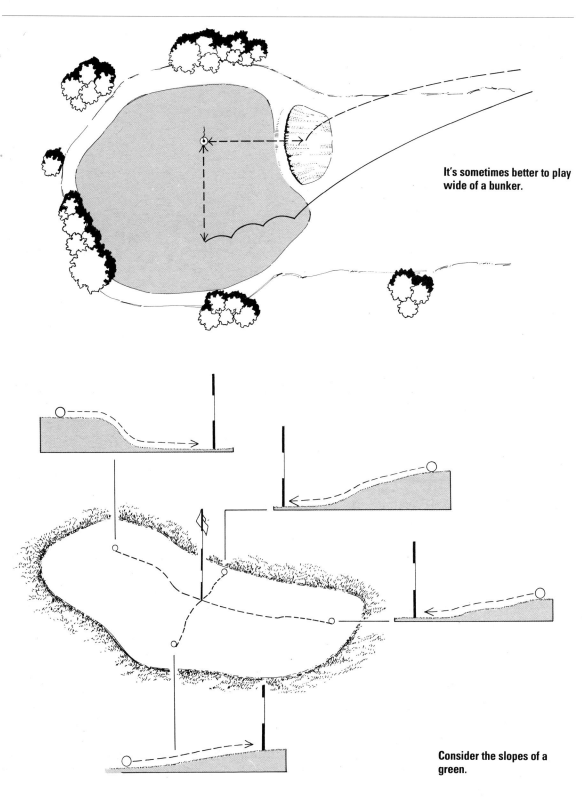

It's sometimes better to play wide of a bunker.

Consider the slopes of a green.

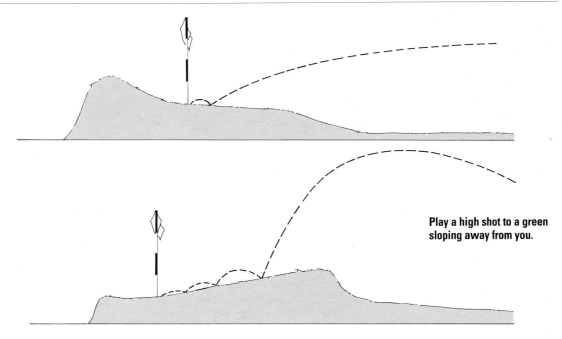

Play a high shot to a green sloping away from you.

water or perhaps even a quarry which must be cleared, or is the trouble, perhaps bunkers, bushes or undergrowth, through the green?

3 Consider the slopes of the green. Think about whether it's better to be left than right, short or long. Obviously you'll be wanting to get your approach shot dead but try to ensure that if you 'fail', you do so in the most favourable direction. You should be aiming at positions where you'll be putting uphill and where there's little contouring.

4 Think of the trouble to the sides of the green. Play away from it unless you're in peak form. It's easier to get down in two putts from fifteen yards than from a bunker or a clump of rough.

5 Think about the height of shot you ought to play. If the green slopes away from you, a high shot will almost always be the best. If you are playing into a slope tilted from back to front a much lower flight will still bite fairly well.

6 Always be sensible about your choice of club. Competent professionals choose the club they believe will give them the right result on the day. All too many good strikers at club level always imagine that they are going to hit their best iron

shot all the time, not their average one. That's why 90 per cent of shots to a flag finish short.

7 Take account of wind, ground and air. Many club golfers decide correctly how much a well-struck shot will run after landing. Into, let's say, a stiff breeze, however, they will only go up one or two clubs when it ought to be three or even four. Be realistic. You are only in any real danger of reaching trouble through the green if you hit one in too low, and therefore under most of the wind.

8 Learn from your many experiences while playing your own course. Some holes will usually give you more trouble than others. A few may have ruined a good round more than once. Take the time to think about it and analyse where you've been going wrong. At worst, work out how to get by them without disaster.

Course management on the putting surface is fairly simple – it's doing it right that's more difficult! (See 'Chipping and Putting'.) Mainly, it's a question of playing the percentages:

1 By all means think in quite firm terms about an uphill putt. You're not so likely to be very far past, and the back of the hole will be a little higher than

139

the front, acting as a backstop – as long as you get your putt on line. You've a better chance of racing it into the hole but remember the more tricky downhiller you may have coming back.

2 If you have a fast downhiller, still try and be positive. It will help if you pick a spot short of the hole and on line. Putt quite firmly to that point, rather than dribble the ball weakly towards the hole itself.

3 On sideslope putts, aim to 'fail' on the top side of the hole, for long putts at least. This gives you the chance of your putt dying into the hole, and if it doesn't your next one will be far shorter. If, however, you are trying to hole a short side-hiller, remember that the harder you hit it the less it will break. If you've got the nerve, you will hole far more with a firm stroke, aiming off very little to right or left of centre. It's so much harder to judge the curl of a dying ball. Alas, you'll also have some nasty ones to hole coming back. I leave the choice to you! I saw that final birdie putt of Seve Ballesteros on the last green at St Andrews in 1984 which make virtually certain he would be the champion. It seemed to be missing all the way but, because it was a dying ball, just toppled in from the side.

4 When any of your putts miss and run past the hole, don't turn away in disgust. Watch the line it takes. This is the best evidence of all for how to aim your next one, so don't throw the chance away.

5 Particularly on a strange course, look at the green as you walk up to it, even from as much as a hundred yards away. You could well have a far better perspective of the slopes from a distance than when you are actually pacing around it.

STROKEPLAY STRATEGY

The majority of club golfers prefer matchplay, especially a fourball, to strokeplay. In a fourball, even when you've had a very bad day indeed, it's possible to convince yourself, perhaps after a few drinks, that you didn't do so badly after all. You remember a vital putt holed or the birdie you made at a crucial stage. Yes, for most of the time you were hardly in the match but can convince yourself you 'came in' when it mattered. Well, what's wrong with that? There is an old saying, 'It takes two to win and one to lose', that used to be applied to foursomes golf but fits the bill for fourballs as well.

However, there are many who argue that medal play is the fairest measure of the man. Club players generally don't like it and regard it as part of the necessary evil of keeping a handicap. In the summer, you may have to enter just to 'get a game' when the summer fixture list seems filled by competitions.

Fear is the main reason for this dislike. How many players dread 'the card and pencil'! They go through the round playing every shot thinking of what might go wrong. They try to steer their drives because all they can see is a mass of trouble to both right and left; for the shot to the green, they are aware of only bunkers and clumps of rough; when they reach the green their minds fill with thoughts of three putts. On the other hand, in fourballs they will very likely need a birdie to win the hole. As a result, they open the shoulders on the drive then go boldly for the hole with both approach shot and first putt.

I must admit that this used to be true of my game. In the summer, we used to play a lot of exhibition matches on Sunday afternoons. Usually it was Dai Rees and David Thomas for Wales with Bernard Hunt and me playing for the honour of England. We did our best, but it really wasn't a matter of life and death. As often as not, we'd be visiting courses we'd not seen before. On the 1st tee, perhaps, we'd say: 'What's the line on this one?'

'Over that tall pine!' or 'Just left of that church spire' might be the reply.

With no fears, we'd swing easily and away our shots flew, following instructions. Later, when we breasted the rise, our drives would be nicely placed in the fairway, but to left and right might be an out-of-bounds, dark impenetrable forest or cavernous bunkers.

It was much the same in the rest of our play. Scorning trouble, we flew our shots at the flag and, once on the green, putted both quickly and boldly. How often they seemed to drop!

As the great American amateur, Frank Stranahan once said: 'In practice you never miss a fairway, get in a greenside bunker or miss a short putt. Then up go the tapes for the real thing and you knock your first one clean out of bounds!'

That's tension and it's something only the greatest players fully get to grips with.

Nevertheless, clear your brain of negative thoughts and go for all the shots you know you can make.

Of course, I'm certainly not talking of taking mindless risks in your medal rounds – that's quite another matter. Decide on the sensible shot to play, visualize the flight and run of a good shot, then step up to your ball and swing.

Keeping a good round going

In professional tournaments, the man who reaches the turn in, say, 31 virtually never scores as well on the way home. He stops attacking the course and thinks mostly about how he mustn't spoil a good card. Those shots can especially leak away on the last few holes. Exactly the same nervous symptoms are found in club golf. How often we hear plaintive cries in the clubhouse:

'I was only four over standing on the 16th tee and then . . .' Or, 'Just had to stick a wedge on the green and two putt, but . . .'

The negative thoughts had taken over, you see. You must be positive. When you're scoring well, tell yourself it's your day. You were meant to win. Try and make it a day to remember. Win by a hatful of strokes. Keep on going for the shots.

If tension does become extreme, compromise by using clubs in which you have real confidence. If you dearly love your 4 iron, why not use it for your last tee shot instead of a wood. Choose your favourite pitching club for that last shot to the green rather than, perhaps, that wedge you've never been fully comfortable with.

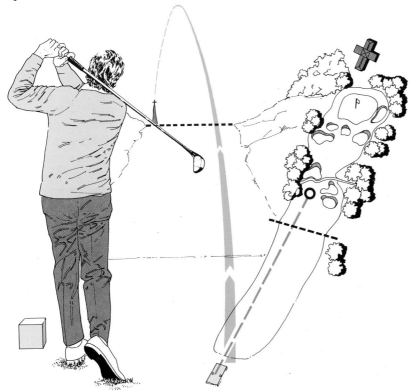

Play with confidence, but if you don't know the course, take advice on the right lines to play because there may be dangers you cannot see.

Above all, keep your swing smooth; complete the backswing and go firmly through the ball, keeping your eye on it till your brain tells you the ball has long gone.

After a poor start

The tip here is 'keep trying'. It may seem obvious, but it's often forgotten by professionals as well as amateurs. Most really bad scores in club competitions are the result of 'giving up'. The player uses up most of his handicap on the first few holes and decides that his driving, putting or whatever are right off. He then throws in the towel.

Don't be that fatalistic. Why not tell yourself instead that, yes, you've hit a few bad shots but that's what your handicap is for. Often you can play well below it. Why shouldn't you begin doing just that right now? Think of Walter Hagen. He always reckoned he was sure to hit four or five poor shots in a round, and it didn't trouble him in the least if they came with a rush at the beginning. His attitude was that he had now got rid of them, and as a result he could still keep his sights on victory.

In more recent times, Gary Player and Jack Nicklaus have never seemed to give up. I think Gary's attitude has always been that if he isn't going to win, then he wants to finish as well up the field as he can manage. How often he's produced a low last round – and sometimes the field has come back to him! With Nicklaus, pride of performance is the key. If victory is well beyond his grasp, he wants to come in with a 68 not a 74. This should apply to club golfers just as much. Isn't it better to come in and say that you were four over your handicap than with a 'no return'?

Remember one final point. We all know how sudden the changes of form can be from day to day and morning to afternoon. This can happen minute by minute as well – but not if you've given up. After a very poor start, you may have little real chance of winning in a medal round but a strong finish will do wonders for your confidence next time out. You'll also have some enjoyment from your round, not total misery.

MATCHPLAY STRATEGY

I wonder if this is a kind of golf in which club golfers are rather more expert than the professionals? Wouldn't that be an enticing thought? After all, at a high competitive level, matchplay is rare and mainly for a select few. There's only the Ryder Cup, the USA versus Japan matches, the fairly new Tucson event that ends the US Tour, the annual World Matchplay at Wentworth, the Epson event at St Pierre in Wales and the Dunhill Cup. Not all of these contests may survive on television because TV is wary of them as it is quite difficult to cope with a vacant hour of transmission time on your hands if every match has finished far from home. Taping earlier play and repeats of other events can't have quite the same drama.

Yet to be realistic, the professionals are still the more experienced even if they seldom seem to play matches. They grew up as golfers playing in a club environment, where matchplay is predominant, and indulge in a great deal of 'friendly' matchplay in practice before tournaments or in the close season.

As regards the basic strategy of matchplay golf, there is one central question. Should you play the course or the man? The philosophy of Bobby Jones, who played far more championship matchplay golf than today's leading players, was always to keep what he called 'Old Man Par' in mind – in other words, play the course. If he could go round in par (in the much more difficult course conditions and with the relatively poor equipment of more than fifty years ago), he'd win.

I think the answer to our question is still simple but not the same: 'Play both.'

You should first aim at playing the course as well as you possibly can, whether your maximum potential is several strokes under par or just to break 100. If you play any match several strokes under your handicap you won't lose all that many of them. Even if you're playing this well, however, there'll be occasions when you really ought to change to the 'playing the man' strategy. They happen when you're on top. Here are a few of them:

1 Your opponent has driven off out of bounds. You do not now try to whistle one away down the middle with your driver. If it's a par 4, he must take four to reach the green. Settle for being as sure as you can to get there in three and play *really* safe from the tee. (No, put away the 4 wood. Hit your 3 iron.) It's very much the same if he has hit into probable trouble or given himself a difficult line into the green. Choose the club (yes, I'll admit it might even be your driver on the day) you think gives you your best chance to put the ball where you want it.

2 Your opponent has bunkered his shot to the green, and his bunker play is no better than average. The chances are that he won't get down in two more. Here, best to think in terms just of getting your approach in within safe two-putt distance. Don't, in order to be dead to the pin, risk trying a shot that will *just* clear a bunker or shave past a tree. Play for a wide part of the green.

3 If both you and your opponent have a twenty footer but his is for a par 4 and yours for a 3, forget the reasonable chance of a birdie and get your putt stone dead. In matchplay there are no medals for birdies. Just win the hole.

These are the three basic situations of golf: the tee shot, the approach and the putting. In each case, the man with the whip hand should think in terms of keeping it.

What, however, of the man who's apparently down and out? His response will, of course, have to be the opposite. He must make his opponent win the hole. There's no strain at all on anyone when a hole is conceded. So keep your hopes eternal. Even when you're out of bounds your next drive could well be a crackerjack and the iron shot stone dead. You emerge with no worse than a bogey 5. It may seem a touch unlikely but my message is, at least try to put some pressure on his nerve. If you seem out of the hole, try to get back into it. You'll halve a few and occasionally win. Above all, you'll increase the stress on your opponent. There's nothing more aggravating in

matchplay than the opponent who just keeps going. Dai Rees and Gary Player were two such terriers. They always seemed to be calling for the referee to ask for relief or consulting the rule book.

However, do concede with good grace when you've knocked three in a row out of bounds or your opponent's ball is scarcely more than a whisker from the hole.

Conceding putts

When, and when not, to concede putts is almost worth a chapter in itself but I'll have to be a bit more concise than that. If your objective is to win the match rather than a new friend, concede very little. In either match or strokeplay I suppose it's rare for one short putt not to be missed somewhere along the way and constant holing-out does increase pressure. The greatest matchplayer of them all, Walter Hagen, had a tormenting tactic. In a 36 hole match he'd concede quite a few of two to three feet in the early stages, then put the screw on at a crisis point. He would even point out how difficult the tiddler was and offer his services to 'help' in lining it up. Because of his legendary charm, defeated opponents seldom seemed to resent his gamesmanship and even told the tale years after. However, I'd advise you to leave these subtleties alone: they could result in serious injury with a testy opponent.

The simple rule is that if you think there's no chance whatsoever of his missing, then sweep up his ball, hand it over courteously and, either by word or gesture, try to leave him with the feeling that you're a generous fellow. But never, never concede a putt he might miss and never if it's to win the match. Also, never assume that you have been given a putt, even if your ball is on the lip. Your opponent is fully entitled to make you pay for so silly an error, one easily made in the heat of the moment.

In general, I believe all those people who have argued that golf is golf and matchplay and strokeplay are really the same game have missed the most important difference.

In strokeplay, you ought to be thinking about returning a good score for 18 holes. In matchplay, you have to think it out hole by hole. Of course, you want to win the lot and depart victorious 10 and 8, but commonsense indicates that you ought to lower your sights a touch. Think of winning each hole, by all means, but also remember not to hand anything to your opponent on a platter. As a result, you have to decide when to play the bold shot and when it's sensible to go on the defensive. What determines your decision is not just the hole but also the overall match situation.

I'll illustrate. Let's suppose you're playing a shortish par 4 when your opponent has played to the green first and is some eight feet from the flag. You are out there with a towering oak overhanging the green and blocking your line in. Do you decide you are capable of flying your wedge over it to skid to a stop at least inside your opponent, or would it be better to prod in a low one wide of the branches that will finish on the green, probably a good deal further away than your opponent's ball is?

In matchplay, your decision should depend on both the state of the match and your thoughts about how your opponent is putting. In strokeplay, your opponent does not exist. You should be considering solely what you're capable of at the time, and your overall score.

In the first instance, you will have to base your decision on how well your opponent is putting. In the second, a medal round, the overall state of your score will come first: are you trying to rescue a poorish score or preserve a good one?

Psychology

So far, we have been looking at what kind of shot your opponent is likely to play at a particular point in the game. What, however, should your more general psychological approach be?

As always in golf, there's no clear-cut answer. Nevertheless, two things stand out in my mind.

I once played Arnold Palmer in a Ryder Cup match when he was at the very peak of his career. Anyone would have been expected to lose against

him, and so did I. As we waited to play at the 1st tee at Royal Lytham in 1961 I was certainly thinking more of the embarrassment of being beaten 6 and 5 than the glory of beating the supreme superstar of that time.

All wrong. I should have been thinking that anything can happen over eighteen holes and that I was in excellent form myself. Sir Walter Simpson's thoughts, written in *The Art of Golf* nearly a century ago, would have given excellent advice:

'It is scarcely ever politic to count the enemy's chickens before they are hatched. Cases constantly occur of holes being lost because it seems absolutely necessary in order to save them to get home from a bad lie. Your forcing shot sends the ball from bad to worse, and what might have been won in five is lost in seven. A secret disbelief in the enemy's play is very useful for matchplay.

'This contempt must, however, be largely seasoned with respect. It does not do lightly to lose the first two holes, or any hole. When one is down it is natural to hunger for holes, but even with five up play greedily for more – play a yard putt as if the match depended on it. Likely enough it will turn out that it did. When five up express, as is polite, regret at laying a stimy,* but rejoice in your heart.'

That far-off day in 1961, things went very well for me. Palmer was not a superman after all, and in the end was a little lucky to halve the match. My mental approach had been wrong – or was it just 1st tee nerves? – but I had got away with it. Perhaps with a more positive approach I would have beaten him.

However, although I'm suggesting you don't think too highly of your opponent's abilities in

---

* The stimy (Sir Walter's spelling) used to be a key feature of matchplay. If, on the putting green, your opponent's ball lay on your line to the hole, you had to get on with it. This meant playing wide, lofting over with a niblick or, worst of all, knocking his ball in.

terms of the match as a whole, as regards the playing of each hole do think him capable of all kinds of magic. At all costs, you must avoid the shock to the nervous system of a hole seemingly in the bag jumping out of it. Providing your shots are straightforward (without undue risks), believe that you must do your very best because your opponent's response is bound to be very good indeed. Also, don't fall into the trap of thinking he's more or less out of the particular hole. Try to produce your best right the way through in case he suddenly plays a wonder shot. Assume, when he looks to be bunkered, that he's not, near bushes not in them, or that his ball will be found just in bounds. Before he plays a particular shot he'll be in the fairway, on the green or hole the putt. This will protect you from a severe shock!

Always remember that in singles matchplay there can be very sudden swings. Never relax when you've got what seems a comfortable lead or give up when you're well down. When you're four up, do your damndest for five. Don't relax until you've shaken hands and said: 'Thank you very much for the game.'

OBSERVATION

Keen observation of how you are playing yourself and how the course is behaving can give you a lot of helpful information.

Tee Pegs

Many old wives' tales have circulated on this subject over the years. For instance, it's often been said that a tee peg flies backwards when a good drive is hit. Well, yes and no – it rather depends on whether the ground is hard or soft. However, it is true that if you are breaking many of them this can be an indication that you are chopping down on the ball, rather than sweeping it away on a level plane. Clubhead strikes ball, ball goes downwards on impact as well as forwards, tee peg can't take the strain. Yet another penny frittered away.

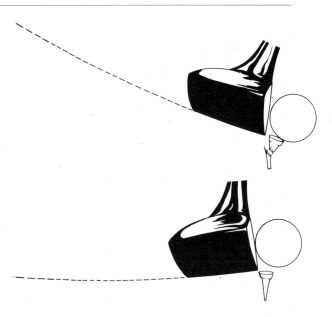

Breaking pegs can be the result of chopping down on the ball.

Golf gloves

Do you often have to buy a new glove? Perhaps you're rather fussy and like yours in pristine condition. (Jack Nicklaus used to reckon to use three new ones a round in humid weather, but that was when the MacGregor company was supplying him with as many as he wanted. Then, a few years ago, Nicklaus bought the firm. He now has reduced his expenditure to one per round, but always a new one.)

However, most golfers buy a new glove only when the old one is worn out. Have a look where it's worn. If you find that the decline has been well-nigh total I'll say no more. However, if it's in this or that part of the glove, there is a simple lesson you can learn: your grip is insecure. The club has been shifting, causing friction and wearing through the thin leather.

This will be either because you are allowing some movement to take place in your backswing, or because there is movement either at or just after impact.

145

You can learn a lot about the way you hold the club from areas of wear on the glove or grip

Grip wear

This is a similar case to wear on the glove and the lessons to be learned are about identical, but the signs do take longer to appear.

Divots

I remember the *Observer* golf correspondent, Peter Dobereiner, wrote an amusing piece on this topic a couple of years ago. He had closely examined the turf on the tee of a par 3 hole after play had ended, and was surprised to find that, for right-handers, the cuts made by the iron heads all went at least slightly from right to left. From this, he deduced that the golf swing of top professionals was not in-to-out but out-to-in.

Well, I can see the logic of his thinking, but there's a little more to it than that. Most very good players do have an in-to-out club path but they seldom relish the thought of hitting hooking iron shots into greens. The ball just doesn't hold at all well unless the ground is soft. They do swing in-to-out but employ various techniques to ensure that they don't get a drawn shape to their iron shots. And one of these is to have the clubhead cutting away at impact. Hence Dobereiner's divots.

For the club golfer and professional alike, however, divots are very helpful in showing just why that shot – never mind if good or poor – went where it did.

Let's look at a few examples.

1 Line of divot strongly in-to-out and ball went further out. The clubface was open to the target at impact, causing slice spin.

2 The same and ball followed the line of divot. Clubface was square to the target line.

3 The same and ball curled with gentle or quick hooking flight. Clubface was closed to the target line at impact.

4 Line of divot strongly out-to-in and ball went straight. Clubface was just slightly closed to the target line at impact. Your slicing swing path was cancelled out by the closed clubface.

5 Same and ball sliced either a little or a lot. Clubface open to the target line. The amount of slice indicates how much.

6 Same and ball followed the line of divot. Clubface was shut to the target line at impact.

However, most golfers will find their divots indicate an out-to-in swing path, the clubhead cutting across the ball. If we go back to Dobereiner's example, we might deduce that the ideal path is out-to-in at impact – but by a very small amount. The divot flies very nearly straight.

Basically, then, they are one of your pieces of evidence about why your ball went where it did: flight of the ball plus line of the divot equals the alignment of your clubhead at impact.

Tell-tale footprints in the sand

Foot prints in the sand tell you about depth, texture and compactness. It's all a very simple

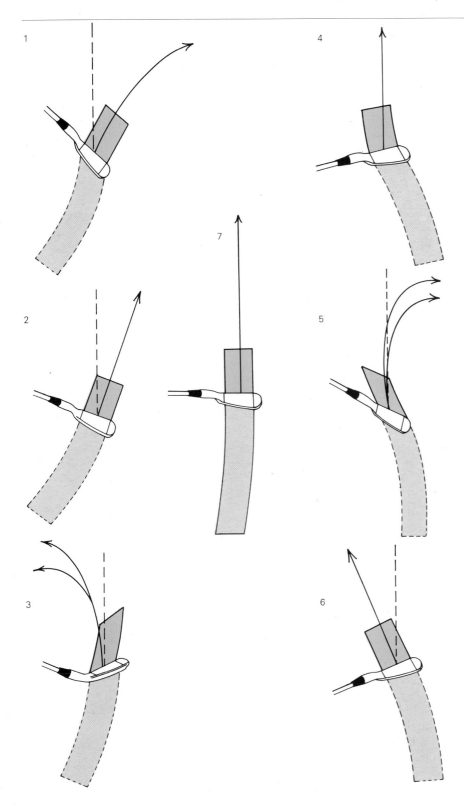

Dobereiner's divots *from top to bottom, left to right: 1* clubhead path in-to-out and the ball went further out; *2* clubhead path in-to-out and the ball followed the line of the divot; *3* clubhead path in-to-out and the ball curved with hooked flight; straight divot and straight ball; *4* clubhead path out-to-in, and the ball went straight; *5* clubhead path out-to-in and the ball sliced; *6* clubhead path out-to-in and the ball followed the line of the divot. What one can learn from these is that in *1* and *5* the clubface was open to the target at impact, in *2* it was square, in *3, 4* and *6* it was closed. In *7* the straight path and straight divot indicate that the club face was square.

matter indeed but the evidence is ignored by really quite good golfers far more than it should be. Of course, everyone notices when they are in wet sand with the footprints sharply outlined and of no great depth. Similarly, it's just as obvious when the sand is extremely soft. The feet leave no distinct impression at all.

It's the in-between zone where the messages from the soles of your feet are most significant.

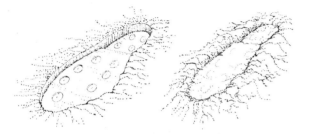

Damp sand registers firm footprints: in soft sand the footprint is less distinct.

There you are in the middle of a bunker. Usually the sand is quite shallow, because bunkers are raked from middle to rear. Wriggle your feet about, trying to sense if this is so, with hard ground no more than an inch below the surface. If it is, it ought to influence your choice of club. Your sand iron may well bounce, and if you're playing a firm shot, your ball will go very much further than you expect, and may even be thinned.

Flight of other players' balls

We're all inclined to wonder what club Jack and Fred have just taken for their shots to the green, especially on a par 3. But even if they hit very much the same length as you with a driver or 3 wood from the tee, this doesn't at all mean that everyone is also going to hit the same distance with, say, a 7 iron. Jack may tend to play with clubhead meeting ball a little ahead of his hands,

Different players using the same club can hit the ball different distances because of variations in their set-up and the amount of clubface they show the ball. Pay more attention then to how the ball flies than to the distance achieved.

set up with the ball opposite his leading instep and tend to have the clubface a touch open at impact. Fred may have the ball positioned well back in his stance, and have the clubface both hooded and closed. The length of shot they then ought to get from a good swing with their respective 7 irons will be very different. Jack makes his into an 8 while Fred reduces the loft on his to that of a 5 iron. So, pay little attention to what club they use and far more to how their shots *fly*. Often, a ball will look as if it's only just going to reach the green, yet there it is, right by a flag set well to the rear. Or the reverse, the ball that appears to be right on line to the flag but finishes many yards short.

These bits of evidence before you play your own shot can be invaluable. They can teach you that the wind around the green is either stiffer or lighter than you thought, or that you may have miscalculated the 'heaviness' or the 'thinness' of the air.

If you do happen to know what clubs your opponents used, let your computer-like brain make allowances for how well or how weakly they struck the ball. If Jack hit the shot of a lifetime and still barely reached the hole, for instance, it's madness to be too confident about your chances of doing the same.

Finally, notice how the ball has run after pitching. Did, for example, the one that came down just a touch short of the green bound on, away and through, while another shot pitched only a yard or two further on and stopped quickly. This ought to tell you that the approaches or apron are hard while the green itself is well-watered and holding. With this evidence, you have alternatives to choose between: the full-at-the-flag shot or a runner pitched short and aimed to skip on towards the flag.

Reading your opponent

I am now going to imagine you in a competitive situation. What I have to say applies just about equally whether you are playing match- or stroke-play, or even in a fourball. We can learn quite a bit about the state of the opposition's nerve by observing not so much their behaviour, as changes in behaviour.

If, for example, your opponent is chain-smoking throughout, walks very fast, has a quick, snatchy backswing or talks quickly and nervously, there may be little to learn from this. It may be his normal behaviour on the golf course and, indeed, in everyday life. If, however, he suddenly starts smoking, or his airy chatter dies away and he retreats into grim silence, this is the time to be encouraged and to redouble your own efforts. Let me give you a few examples from the golfing past.

The event that caused the first golf boom in the USA was the play-off for the 1913 US Open fought out by Harry Vardon, the man who still holds the record for the most British Opens won (six), Ted Ray, then current British Open champion, and Francis Ouimet, a twenty-year-old shop assistant with a very slim record indeed in American amateur golf. Naturally, Ouimet was not given a chance of beating the great men. However, he managed to hang on over the first nine holes and went ahead on the 10th. Even so, he still had no real expectations of winning. Then, on the 15th, he saw Vardon take out a pipe and fumble on lighting it. Ouimet realized that the seemingly imperturbable Vardon was also made of human clay, was vastly encouraged and went on to win very comfortably indeed. What had especially lifted him was that he had heard Harry Vardon never smoked at all on the golf course. Not true, but . . .

Probably no man ever gave away less emotionally in golf than Ben Hogan. He met good and bad bounce, the short putt missed or the long curving ones holed, equally impassively. Even so, Sam Snead tells a story about the play-off for the 1954 US Masters. They reached the par 3 16th with Snead holding a narrow one-stroke lead. Both tee shots found the green with Hogan some six yards away and Snead about three yards further.

Snead decided to make sure of getting his long approach up to the hole, and did so. Hogan's normal deliberate putting behaviour suddenly changed drastically. He sent the putt away with scarcely a pause, with a much shorter and jerky backswing than usual, and mishit it to boot. Inevitably, his ball finished short, and inevitably he missed the next one. Snead was able to play out the championship serenely. He knew he had his man on the run, and this increased his confidence.

Earlier in his career, although one of the best two or three American players right from his first appearance in tournament golf, Snead couldn't win a major championship and had thrown away the 1939 US Open by taking an 8 on the last hole.

However, in 1942 he fought through to the final of the US PGA (then a matchplay event), where he met Jim Turnesa.

Turnesa held a 3-up lead after 23 holes, but after four more holes the match was level. Snead watched his man closely as Turnesa prepared to drive on the next. Before he swung, Turnesa usually took a couple of wiggles followed by a slight forward press. This time, he had about five, followed by a much jerkier foward movement. Away into the woods his ball went and Snead knew he had broken his man.

Very early in his career Bobby Locke decided to be as impassive as possible. He didn't want an opponent to know when he was 'hurt'. He did, however, very much want to know when they were and observed them closely. He found he was much encouraged when playing with someone who needed to smoke, especially if the tobacco consumption rose from an ocasional one to as much as three per hole. One top American, he found, could not stand still when his back was to the wall, while another scratched himself nervously. Perhaps the oddest example was the reaction of one player. Whenever Locke holed a long putt, a white line some half an inch wide would appear down his cheek. Well, I'm afraid there was nothing he could do about that!

During my own playing career I always tried to show no emotion at all. This, naturally, was particularly true of matchplay. If you look upset when your opponent holes a long putt you give him a lift. He feels that you've been shaken even when you haven't, and may well play better as a result. So, whether 4 up with 6 to play, or 4 down, I tried to be impassive. It's much easier than trying to fake emotions to fit the circumstances.

Learning from others

Finally, observation is always a way of learning. Watch the people you play with. Never mind if old George plays off 19 and will never be any lower. Obviously he has plenty of weaknesses in his game but there may be a strength or two as well. Perhaps he's a miracle worker when chipping with a 7 iron. Try to see why, and if you can't don't be shy of asking. He'll probably be immensely flattered.

Similarly, some players are exceptionally good from sand in your own club. Ask them how they think they do it and then form your own conclusions from what you see yourself.

My father told me to look and learn. I heeded his words as a teenager and I'm still doing it.

BEATING THE WEATHER

Heat

Many golfers, especially those used to playing in bracing or cold conditions, allow hot weather to affect their play far more than they should.

Don't, for instance, walk at a snail's pace. You won't feel any cooler and you'll be out under the hot sun that much longer. Instead, maintain a normal crisp pace.

Choose suitable clothes. The shoes should be your loosest not tightest pair, with leather soles preferable, if you have them. Trousers should not be tight and, of course, as light a weight as you have. Much the same applies to shirts, with cotton very much preferable to any artificial material. If it's not just hot but very sunny as well, don't play in a short-sleeved shirt if your arms are not tanned, and it's not a bad idea to choose a shirt with a collar which stays up to protect the back of the neck. Also avoid shorts. If your eyes find bright sunlight a strain, have a cap or tennis eye-shade with a long peak to hand. For the extremely sensitive, sun-glasses are a very good idea, though you could find it a little more difficult to follow the flight of the ball, while some find the ball looks to be in a slight depression at address. Sun-glasses also seem to help hay fever sufferers and sun stroke too – a doctor friend tells me that this is usually caused by too much light in the eyes.

Make use of whatever shade there is on the course. There is unlikely to be much but look around you, especially when waiting to play a tee shot during a hold-up in play. Use your umbrella.

Some of us have sweatier hands than others, which can prevent one gripping the club with full confidence. Have a small hand towel available at all times. You will need it for rain anyway. A good-sized piece of chamois leather is even better, if more expensive.

Dehydration can be a problem in extreme heat and, even when it isn't a danger, many golfers like to have a drink with them. In temperate climates it certainly isn't physiologically necessary, but do what suits you best. I'd advise against sweet drinks, which don't quench the thirst as well as something sharper in taste. I wouldn't rule out cold tea or water.

Above all, however, don't allow heat to take a psychological hold on you. Remember that golfers go out in the midday suns of Kuala Lumpur and West Africa where there is high humidity to cope with as well, and also the sheer temperatures of countries as Libya, Egypt and Saudi Arabia when it is frequently more than 100°F in the shade.

Cold

I've known a few golfers at club level who seem to be at their best in a biting wind at 8 o'clock on a Sunday morning when a hard frost has made a normal pitch to a green the most stupid shot of all to play. Often these are fellows not blessed with a rhythmically powerful golf swing but they do have touch. They are able to sense and judge how the ball will run and adjust accordingly. I suspect they are also blessed with unusually good circulation!

Of course, it's not the low number of degrees on the thermometer that's the main consideration but any added wind – 'the chill factor'.

More clothing is required to combat cold plus wind, than for cold by itself. In either event, however, the dilemma is to be warm but not so heavily clothed that you can get nowhere near a full backswing. Furthermore, many players find they are distracted by the rustling of waterproof jackets, but a closely woven fabric of this type will keep the wind out better than any amount of wool. Developments in waterproof clothing in recent years have anyway much reduced the problem.

A little thought before going out on a very cold day can pay dividends. Many golfers have come to find thermal underwear a must. It is light and allows the player to do away with at least one and maybe two layers of more cumbersome outer garments.

A hat or cap of some kind is also essential unless you have a very thick head of hair. Keep your extremities warm and the rest will take care of itself. I think it's been calculated that we lose about 20 per cent of body heat via the head. If buying your head gear just for winter golf, remember it needs to be able to withstand a shower of rain and not be liable to wheel away down the fairway with every gust of wind.

Shoes are also important. Ideally what we require are ones that are waterproof (or at least water resistant) and not cold and clammy. On this count, most people will want to use rubber shoes when the ground is fairly waterlogged while the man-made material, though waterproof, is apt to blister delicate feet. Soft leather uppers are very comfortable and perhaps best for summer wear but are seldom very water-resistant. That suppleness means thinness too. However, in my opinion, for 'average' winter conditions, by which I mean cold with the ground wet underfoot but not a quagmire, shoes with fairly stiff leather uppers are practically ideal. Leather soles are far warmer than composition or rubber but they suffer in wet conditions. This tendency can be lessened if you give the soles a careful coating in a waterproof polish each time they get a thorough soaking.

Finally, while I'm on the subject of footwear, thick soles mean that you've got more insulation between the soles of your feet and the cold, cold ground and, if you keep to the fairways, your uppers are not in contact with wet grass. The old toffs of my Ferndown years used to play in highly polished Veldtshoens which looked adequate for the Himalayas. All the better if they can accommodate two, even three pairs of socks.

Boots are not recommended except for warmth. They restrict ankle movement and, no matter what the adverts say, do allow your feet to move inside the boot. Keep them only for when the ground is wet and muddy.

As regards trousers, the denser the fabric (*not* thicker) the better, and a light pair of water- and windproof ones will amply take care of the golfing person below the waist.

Above the waist we want to keep as free a shoulder turn as possible and also prevent the arms from feeling constricted. Fortunately, the arms need less covering than the torso. Therefore, equip yourself with two or three pullovers, but short-sleeved rather than long-sleeved. Make sure that at least one of these has a round or, better still, roll neck collar. Rely on wool to combat cold, and use a windproof jacket only when strictly necessary, unless you have found that you're happy in one. Sleeveless jackets are excellent.

Golfers with poor circulation in their feet and hands find playing in cold weather particularly difficult. They should keep themselves moving, but still need extra protection. A pair of down-filled ski mittens to don between shots are the best hand covering available, though woollen will do fairly well. A charcoal-burning hand-warmer is also useful, though you really need two, one for each pocket, and then the whole thing becomes rather cumbersome. The simple, if inelegant, ruse of keeping hands in pockets the maximum possible is simple and costs nothing.

For the actual hitting of shots in cold weather, remember that a cold ball flies a shorter distance and allowance must also be made for heavier air.

These two factors mean that you should use at least two clubs more for the same distance through the air in winter than on a clear day in summer day.

In the wind

The problems of playing in wind are much the same whatever the temperature. Perhaps the first essential is to recognize that you are unlikely to play up to your normal standard in very strong winds. The ball travels a shorter distance into the wind, and is less easy to control downwind, while cross winds bring judgement and exact striking more strongly into play. But it's the same for everyone and the player who accepts that he will score less well is already ahead of most of the competition.

If you're going to achieve anything near your normal length *against the wind* you must keep the ball low. A normal well-struck drive has considerable backspin on it, and the harder it is struck into wind the more it will soar up. As a tournament player, my own method was to move the ball back a couple of inches in my stance, hit smoothly and more easily and keep my hands ahead of the clubhead at impact, sometimes using a 2 wood so that I could turn the toe in. I have known other players, that fine Argentine golfer of the 1940s and 1950s, Tony Cerda, for instance, who hit the ball a little thin at will, aiming for a point of contact just above the equator. Beware, when moving the ball back in your stance, of hitting down at it, for this will have quite the opposite result from what is wanted – the ball will fly higher than your normal drive. You must still sweep it away, coming into the ball with your clubhead on line with ball and target and no suggestion of a chop down at the ball.

Severiano Balesteros has the opposite prescription for driving into the wind. He moves the ball *forwards* from its normal driving position to only just inside the toecap. His thinking here is that he wants to avoid hitting *down* most of all. That move a couple of inches forwards means that he feels he can contact the ball with his clubhead

Hitting into the wind: *from top to bottom* normal drive, moving ball back a couple of inches, deliberately hitting thin, hitting down, and moving ball forwards.

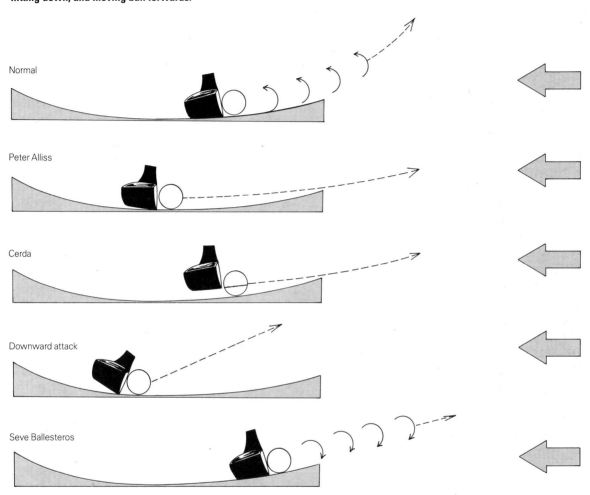

Normal

Peter Alliss

Cerda

Downward attack

Seve Ballesteros

slightly on the rise. He also, like me, grips down the shaft an inch or so and takes a shorter backswing. This is to increase control and therefore accuracy of striking. As John Jacobs says, 'Don't try to hit it harder. Hit it better.' These shots are far more affected in flight into a head wind when, for example, a fairly gentle fade can become a wild, slice.

It has been calculated that a 200 yard drive in still air will travel 300 yards with a 20 mph following wind. A shot into the same wind speed will travel just 133 yards. When driving to a fairway, all that happens in either case is that the ball goes a certain number of yards, leaving you nearer to or further from the green. But think how much more vital the wind factor becomes for a shot to the green. I'll leave it to you to work out the dramatic effect on club selection, but it does mean that if you can hit a 1 or 2 iron around the 200 yard mark in still air, you'll be some fifty or sixty yards short of the green with the same club when hitting into a stiff breeze.

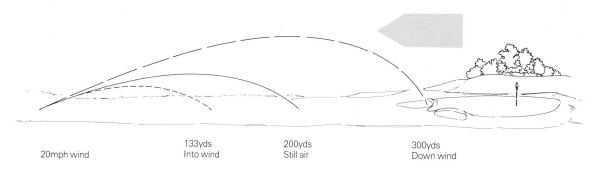

	133yds	200yds		300yds
20mph wind	Into wind	Still air		Down wind

Yet many golfers, when playing a par 3 into wind, fail to take enough club. If they normally use a 7 iron, they perhaps move up to a 6, whereas a much straighter-faced iron, perhaps a 4, is the right choice.

As often as not then, take a stronger club than you really think you need and concentrate your thoughts mainly on achieving good smooth contact while swinging firmly but not flat out.

When playing *downwind*, we want to get the ball up high. This helps it float along and also reduces backspin so that it runs further on landing. Unless your normal drive produces a rather high ball anyway, you will get more distance from the tee using, say, a 3 wood because of the higher flight.

Remember to calculate that certain hazards – say a stream or a fairway bunker – may suddenly come into range, and if so you will have to play short. It may be flattering to your ego to be able to boast that you were in the stream from the tee at the 12th but it's still a stroke wasted, not at all clever.

Approach shots can be tackled in three very different ways. One is to accept that you will not be able to work as much backspin on the ball and therefore to play short, allowing the ball to run the last part of its journey but still playing a basically high shot. Another is to try to minimize the wind effect by playing a low runner – perhaps a little push with a 5 iron when in still air you would be striking a 9 iron or wedge to the flag. This is the best kind of shot for those players – an increasingly rare breed in the days of watered greens – who are happy at the pitch and run. Finally, if you are striking the ball very well on the day you can still

When playing a shot from the fairway to the green a headwind can have a dramatic effect on the distance you achieve.

virtually go for the flag if the greens are holding. Instead of the wedge, perhaps take your sand iron and hit crisper and harder. That following wind will take your ball about a 9 iron distance through the air. From the clubface, your ball will have considerably more backspin, much of which will still be there, despite the wind, when your ball hits the green. However, I am not a believer in forcing iron shots, and don't advise you to play this kind of shot unless your swing is in very good working order.

As with playing downwind there is no single simple way to tackle a *cross wind*. For instance, that very rare bird, the pure straight hitter, can merely allow for a little loss of length and his ball will deviate very little indeed on the wind, provided that it has no sidespin.

However, almost all high-class professionals aim to play with either draw or fade, a majority the latter, although they are capable of reversing their pattern of flight. If you have this level of ball control the options are open, as follows.

When you are driving, if the wind is blowing into your body, a drawn ball will run much further – but perhaps into trouble. If you work it into the cross wind with a fade, you will lose some length but your drive will more or less stay where you land it. This, then, is the 'professional' safe drive played, when you want all the length you can get to make the stroke to the green easier, but not at the risk of losing control. There are, of course, exceptions to this golden rule. By all means 'use' the wind for more length if you see a chance to get up

154

in two at a par 5 or the stroke index 1 par 4, but weigh up the perils first. A different shot is needed when hitting to the green. I think Tom Watson's magnificent 2 iron to the last green at Royal Birkdale will long remain in my memory as an example of skilful play in a cross wind. Watson worked the ball into the wind, hitting, he says, a slight draw as it was blowing from left to right. The result was a shot just about dead straight, the two spin effects cancelling each other out.

The other method, of course, is to allow for the drift of the ball on the wind, with the sidespin more or less doubled. However, when your ball lands on the green it will usually run more sharply sideways and you will need to have judged the landing point very exactly indeed. Normally, the Watson approach – if you can work the ball both ways – is the better of the alternatives.

Though many players are more concerned about the wind effect on their long shots, a strong wind on a green is a problem for which there is just no answer sometimes.

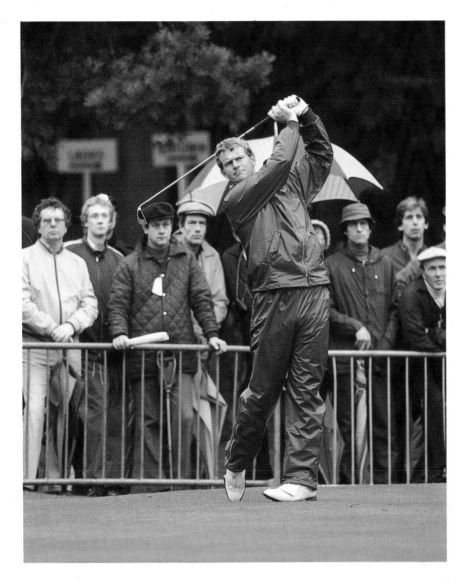

Sandy Lyle dressed for the wet – one of the few players who seem to be happy playing in a full set of waterproofs, as was shown in recent Opens.

The effects of side wind.

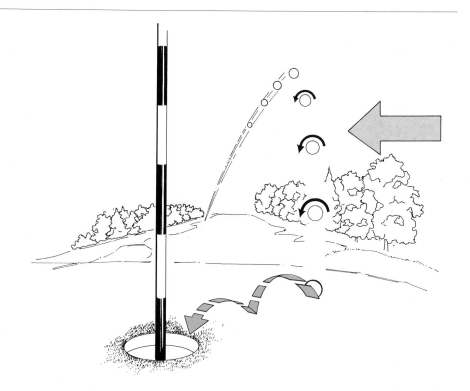

For instance, if you are putting downwind, downhill and with the grain running your way on a very fast green you'll just have to hole the putt – or hope for the best! You may even need to think of putting away from the hole, which makes the game a farce. However, this isn't likely to happen often. When it does, take your medicine as calmly as you can – others will be suffering too.

Make up your mind about strength and line before you take up your stance. Set your feet a little wider apart. Some people also find that a shorter backswing and a firm rapping stroke more effective. If you sense that there is a danger of your ball moving, don't ground your putter head; that way you'll avoid that one-stroke penalty. Don't dawdle, but make use of any drop in wind speed. In the brief lull, move quickly into your stance and send the putt away. Easier said than done, I know. It's almost possible to be bowled over a strong wind even when braced against it.

When you're calculating borrow and strength, make an allowance for the wind, but remember that the main effect of the wind is on you rather than the ball. It's only on very fast greens that wind has a very marked effect. Then, a gentle curve of putt with the wind helping the borrow can make a great difference.

Although I have been talking about the effect of the wind on the *ball*, its unbalancing of the body is just as important – if not even more so. A wind blowing into the player's back tends to push him towards the ball and increases any tendency to slice. One solution is to make every effort to play quickly. Try to take up your stance between gusts and don't dally over the ball. The tension will rise and balance will become even more difficult if you take a long time. Widen your stance a little and shorten your backswing. Finally, be aggressive. Lack of confidence in the wind causes more bad shots than any other single factor. Grip firmly.

Rain

There really is no substitute for a good caddie if you have to play in a downpour. A lone golfer can't hope to keep both himself and his equipment dry without outside help in prolonged heavy rain when the wind is blowing at anything above a light breeze.

However, you can hope to keep your game together without a caddie if conditions aren't too severe – if you prepare sensibly. The essentials are to keep your hands and grips dry, for while it is highly uncomfortable to be soaked to the skin it should not in itself destroy your ability to put a good round together.

Make sure that you always keep your bag hood zipped up. You can hang a towel from the spokes of your golf umbrella, with a spare in a waterproof pocket of your bag. Most car drivers rely on chamois leather to clear misted windscreens, because it's far more effective at absorbing moisture than cotton, and you can learn from them. Have a generous piece in your pocket, reserving it for the final drying of a club grip when the towel has absorbed most of the moisture.

Some of the new golf gloves are especially good in the wet so if you have a pair keep them neatly wrapped in your bag for when they are really needed. Some people consider artificial suede or simple white cotton gloves the best for the rain. I've tried them all, and they work.

Once you have attended to the hands and grip it does help if the rest of you is reasonably comfortable. The umbrella is the first line of defence but waterproof suits have improved enormously in recent years. They used, in my young days, to be little more than wind-cheaters built to withstand only light showers, and were rather stiff and heavy. Now you can get suits that will keep you dry in all but the foulest weather. But to retain their water-resistant properties they have to be looked after, so hang them up to dry after use. The worst possible treatment is to leave them scrunched up in your golf bag, nor is it much better to chuck them into the boot (trunk) of your car and then pile bag and trolley on top of them. You don't want them to crack when dry because they are full of creases, nor for the seams to get stretched and then let in water.

A hat or cap which doesn't immediately become saturated in heavy rain, as cotton jockey caps do, is also a must. Once your hair is thoroughly soaked, the only place for the water to go is straight down your neck. Not the most comfortable situation for playing a round of golf!

Spectacle wearers have special difficulties in rain. A cap or tennis visor with a very long peak is some help but there's still no substitute for being equipped with lots of lens tissue, as Hale Irwin knows full well.

Although it's not as important as what it does to you, rain also affects the flight and run of the ball. The moisture content of the air will be higher and colder. To counterbalance this, allow for your shots flying less far. Take more club and err on the side of over-clubbing unless there are serious hazards just through the green.

How much the run of the ball is affected depends very much on the softness of the ground, and some players find that they score better in winter than summer. Golf often becomes a less subtle game then, and judgment of the amount of run you will get with a shot into the green is not greatly tested. You can fly the ball all the way to the flag and be sure that it will stop quickly – even with a 3-wood.

Especially when playing pitch shots, aim to 'be up'. A rule of thumb is, think in terms of aiming at the top of the flag. This should help overcome the normal dry-weather habit of always playing a little short.

There is not much difference between summer and winter in this respect, except that everything becomes more extreme when the air is colder and the ground softer.

Finally on weather, whatever your own particular bugbear – whether it's bright sun, a stiff breeze, or the fact that you think you can't feel the club at all when your hands are chilled – resolve that you're at least going to try to beat it. An even better attitude is to see bad weather as a competitive advantage to you. Go out properly equipped and with the right mental attitude, and let others flounder.

PRACTICE ROUTINES

In team games you have to practice. There is pressure on you to do so – you just do not get picked unless you show that you are good enough. Fortunately for people in these sports, practice is often part of the fun: at the beginning of the season there are old faces to see again, and there is time for relaxing together after the rigours of the session.

Even in individual games practice involves other people. In tennis and squash you at least need someone to hit the ball back at you. In golf, on the other hand, practice is usually done alone, and for this reason at least 90 per cent of club golfers seem to dislike it so much that they never hit a golf ball except in actual play or while waiting on the putting green.

However, there is no substitute for some (not too arduous) off-course routines. This is true even if you manage to play almost all the daylight hours of the year, and especially so if you play only once or twice a week. However, there is little point in just randomly hitting balls by the hundred on the practice ground, so the following remarks have been written with dedicated non-practisers in mind.

UNDER COVER

If you're prevented from playing by bad weather or lack of time, or simply have a few idle moments, there are a surprising number of little checks and drills you can do under cover.

Jimmy Demaret used to tell a tale of Ben Hogan that illustrates this. One night he woke up in his hotel room to hear a dull thudding from the next-door room. He glanced at his watch. It was 3 a.m. Hogan was still at work trying to iron out a putting problem. He had gone upstairs to his room immediately after dinner to work on some advice on putting that Byron Nelson had given him. The hours passed and Hogan didn't cease his pursuit of perfection. He was not alone in this respect for most tournament players have benefited from indoor routines.

Practising indoors against a wall forces you to swing the putter straight.

All indoor practice should be simple. The aim is to get the mechanics right and build up your confidence. It is very different from actual play; indoors it's the mechanics you concentrate on.

Putting

Some of the mechanics of your putting stroke can be checked far better indoors than out. Use a full-length mirror to check your grip, ball position and posture. See if you are taking the blade back square or inside the line. If you add a ball, you can also see if you're bringing the blade in square at impact and following through along the right path.

You can find out if you're committing the very common error of pushing your blade away from you as you swing back from the ball by using a straight piece of furniture or the botttom of a wall. Face up to your ball with putter toe perhaps an

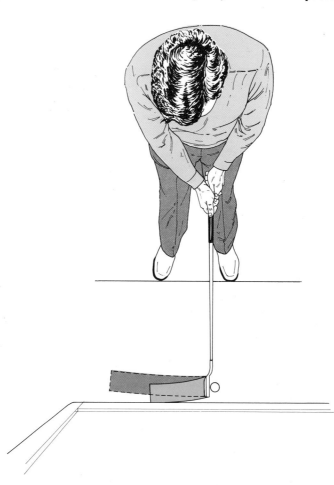

inch or less away from the woodwork. It will collide almost immediately with the wall if you're taking it back outside the line. Work on your putting stroke, then come back and see if the action has been corrected.

You can also putt against that wall. One of the most important factors in good putting is a consistent strike, so you can putt against the wall (a cushion against it will be quieter) and forget all about a target. Just listen for, and feel, a really solid strike. Swing the putter gently back and through. Think, swing and strike.

The importance of concentrating on striking the ball well has been supported by other players, for example John Stirling and George Archer.

John Stirling is one of the best British coaches. He had become just as desperate as I sometimes used to on the greens. Having decided to simplify things as much as possible on short putts, he just squared his 4½-inch blade to the 4½-inch diameter hole, and followed by thinking solely of bringing the middle of the blade into contact with the ball. These 'simple' objectives helped him to get rid of negative thoughts. He banished all ideas of holing out or missing and just thought of the actions involved far more than the actual target.

I also talked recently with George Archer, US Masters champion in 1969 and still a US Tour winner in 1984. I'd certainly rate him in the top half dozen of the last twenty years on the greens. He maintained that, once you were more than three feet or so from the hole, a poorly struck putt never seems to go into the hole. The ball just wanders or dribbles away to left or right. Maybe sometimes it finds its way in like a blind hog looking for an acorn but such happy chances are definitely few and far between.

Therefore, only when you feel satisfied with your striking, add a target. For a while, think only of line, not strength as well. Aim, say at the leg of a table. My bet is you'll be amazed how often you hit it. Your strike is good and you haven't yet added decisions about strength to your problems.

Soon, it may be time to calm down if you're becoming too excited by your own brilliance.

Pick a spot on your carpet, and putt to and over it, trying to stop your ball just a very few inches past. Of course, bear in mind that your living room carpet can be either much slower or faster than a real-life green.

If this seems rather simple, there is something more sophisticated. Many home putting devices have been marketed over the years, and very good some of them are. They range from those which are a simple indoor substitute for the hole to much more expensive ones, which often aim to reproduce the surface of a green.

On one I endorsed some years ago you could change the slope and line and also make your own personal green fast or slow. This was done by brushing the nap towards you for a slow putt and away for the fast ones. All in all, it was ideal for practising the two- to eight-footers. At the end of the session you just folded it up and stowed it away.

There are others which can be rolled up after use and can also be used for chipping practice. Keep an eye on the adverts in golf magazines, especially at Christmas time. You'll come across the one that suits both your pocket and your home conditions.

Chipping and pitching

With chipping and pitching at home be wary. Even the mini-swing of the chip and little pitch needs a touch more clubhead speed than putting and it's entirely possible to thin, shank or top one into the glass-fronted family heirloom or squirt one through the brand-new TV set. So do keep your swing very mini indeed. It's sensible to use light plastic balls.

As with putting indoors, it's the mechanics and feel of the shot rather than a target that you should think about first. Again make use of a full-length mirror if you've got one, to check out grip and alignment. Note your hand position in relation to the clubhead. Very few players can chip even moderately if they have their hands behind the clubhead at impact. They may manage a few good ones from time to time but the odds are stacked

Chipping is rarely effective with the hands behind the ball at impact.

against them, and heavy and thin ones will be far more frequent.

For chipping, work on the mechanics of good striking. Admittedly this is much more difficult than with putting. Whatever club you are using, there is more loft on the clubhead, so find the ideal ball position and work on having your hands a consistent distance ahead of the ball. Once you've worked that out satisfactorily, a short chip is not that much different from a longish putt, except that a little of the travel is through the air.

It is also well worth altering your chipping surface. A fluffy carpet is at least a little like chipping a ball that is lying well down in grass, and if a bare lie frightens you, why not nip into the kitchen to try to build up confidence by working on the smooth floor or, better still, the flagstones of your ancestral home. Seeing the sparks fly should concentrate the mind wonderfully!

This is not a bad time to experiment with grips. If you use a reverse overlap for putting, you may find it will work well for chipping too. Jack Nicklaus

felt he became a better chipper when he learned to view the stroke basically as a long putt played a little more firmly with a more lofted club and the reverse overlap grip.

Above all, however, a bad chipper is someone who cannot strike this gentle shot consistently. Build up confidence at home when your own course is snow-bound or waterlogged. Or just in those few spare moments.

The biggest real golf shot you can play at home is the pitch, and only the very short pitch at that – in fact, the sort of length involved when you want to loft the ball over a bunker to a flag set just beyond it, or to clear a patch of grass to the front edge of a green. Again, it's feel and confidence you should be working to build. This time you will have no precise target for the finishing point of the ball, and you would play towards a soft-backed armchair or a sofa. Make a particular part of the object your target. Practise landing the ball near the spot time and time again with, for example, a 9 iron.

Although seldom used for approach shots nowadays, it's also possible to note just how much height you will get quite quickly even on a club as straight-faced as a 5 iron. Though you are never going to be trying to play short pitches with this particular club, it can be very useful on occasion to play a long-running pitch shot into a stiff wind instead of punching a full wedge into the air and see it blown to oblivion.

The cut up shot

In 'real life', that is, out on the course, this really is a do-or-die shot, because you have to lay the blade so far open – much more often a do-*and*-die one. It's used from a short distance when you want to loft the ball as vertically as possible and reduce run to the absolute minimum. It's remarkable how hard you can hit for all the force is dissipated by cut and backspin. It goes up, not forwards. The side spin enables you to aim away from the hole, calculating that the ball will run sideways towards it. The trouble is that we're almost out of the realms of the mini-swing: the shot is played quite forcefully. The force is dissipated by laying the face of a wedge or 9 iron wide open and then cutting across the line of flight – all rather like a

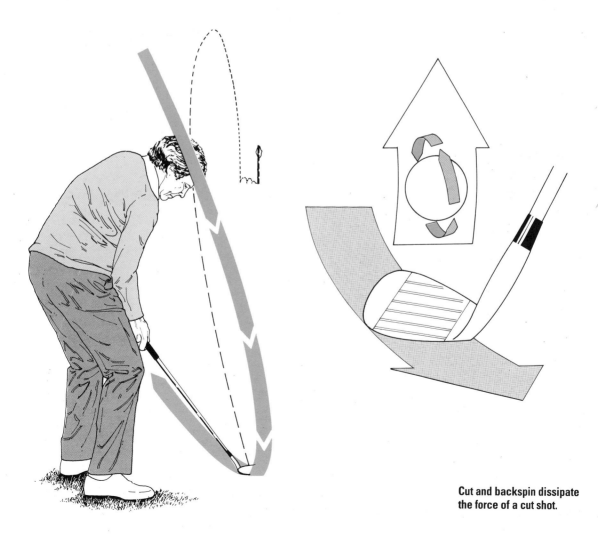

Cut and backspin dissipate the force of a cut shot.

163

standard splash bunker shot, but more so. The wrists break very early.

Indoors, obviously, you do not use a real golf ball but a plastic one. It can be fun to try to see how near the vertical you can make it fly, perhaps hitting the ceiling a few feet ahead of your stance.

The full swing

Your main aim with practising the full swing should be to keep your golfing muscles in trim, to keep muscle memory going. The feel of the golf swing can be lost in a few days, and although there is no real substitute for the feel of clubhead meeting ball, swinging at home does at least preserve some of that feel. If you can only play at weekends or if bad weather is keeping you off the course, keep swinging. Waggle the club and write your signature in the air to preserve feel of the club-head.

Indoors also provides the opportunity to experiment. Perhaps there is a swing fault you are very conscious of, such as too fast a backswing or hitting from the top. Swinging without the fear of actually mishitting a golf ball may well give you a more relaxed approach. But do try out any change in your method before actually putting it to the test on the course. Any new-found confidence you have developed will be gone with the wind if your first stroke is a poor one.

In garage or cellar

One of the problems of indoor practice is that often there just isn't enough space or ceiling height to enable a full swing, and even if there is that vital element of striking a golf ball is absent. However, don't despair – there may well be an alternative.

When he lived in Spain, Severiano Ballesteros had to put up with a poor winter climate. In his part of the north of the country he may not have had much snow to contend with, but he lived on a coast that gets a lot of rain. Seve did, however, have a large cellar. There he rigged up simple matting and hit his ration of full shots into it to keep his muscles supple and hands lively.

Henry Cotton, when he was a fledgling professional in his late teens at the Langley Park Golf Club, used to do much the same thing in his garage. However, there wasn't quite enough roof height for him to swing fully back and that's why he emerged as a great player with a relatively short backswing, in fact a three-quarter one.

If you also have a suitable garage or cellar, you can equip it without expensive equipment. One or two old double mattresses, blankets, canvas or old fishing nets suspended from the roof will do very well. But make sure that there aren't too many breakables about for when the occasional mishit occurs.

If your house has neither garage nor cellar, you might rig up a practice net in the back garden. But if you do this it is dangerous to trust yourself never to miss something that's not specifically made for the job, for one ball into the neighbour's dining room would probably put an end to your practice for ever. A proper net will not cost a lot and will last for a long time. Remember, however, to inspect it for damage from time to time. You can wear it away if you are a consistent striker.

ON THE PRACTICE GROUND

As a tournament player I used to come in for my fair share of criticism for 'not practising enough' but in reality I never undervalued its importance. Before the Carnoustie Open Championship of 1968 it was reported that I had not once been seen on the practice ground, but what the writer didn't know, and didn't trouble to find out, was that I chose to warm up on a nearby course, as I preferred being away from the hustle and bustle of the crowds.

As regards practice routines, professional golfers vary enormously. At one extreme, there is Ben Hogan. It was normal for him to go round several strokes under par and then depart to the practice ground for a matter of hours. My dear old friend, the late Jimmy Demaret, once said how he came upon Hogan hitting 3 woods by the hour. To Demaret's opinion that such dedication to one club was hardly necessary, Hogan replied, 'I want to find out how I play the club when I'm tired.'

Few would give you an argument if you said that the great American spent more hours on the practice tee than anyone before or since, though Gary Player ran him close.

At the other extreme, we have Walter Hagen, who would not admit to practising at all, often arrived late at the first tee, and said that many players left their best golf on the practice ground. However, Hagen enjoyed creating myths about himself. He did practise, especially early and late in his career, and didn't stay up as late or drink as many whisky sours as was thought – rather like Doug Sanders years later.

Of the moderns, Johnny Miller, in his great days did little work. He felt his game was best suited to a short, gentle warm-up and no more.

Indeed, the great players of yesteryear almost to a man believed that simply playing a lot of golf was the best practice of all. But Byron Nelson and Hogan in America and Henry Cotton in Britain changed all this. They were the first great players to practise seriously, and it seems to be believed nowadays that every tournament player must put in many hours weekly, even daily.

So amongst the top players it seems that some practise to the point of exhaustion, others feel they can maintain form best with very little, preferring to do no more before a competitive round than strike a few balls to loosen up and get the feel of clubhead meeting the ball. However, do not be deceived, for this latter group already have swings moulded long, long ago. As youngsters, they practised for hours, but once the swing was established they found it suited them better, and maintained a more competitive edge, if they did not hit golf balls away by the hundred, perhaps working into a fault rather than away from one.

Jack Nicklaus, for example, considers that his own swing has remained fundamentally unchanged since the age of thirteen, although, of course, he has introduced, rejected and reintroduced once again many little modifications. Much the same is true of me. In my case, I did find it necessary to change my grip drastically at the age of fifteen, but the ways the shoulders turned, arms folded and straightened and legs worked were well set long before that. Of course, I did experiment, especially with the take-away: hands and arms together, and the opposite, a quick wrist break.

A common and justified complaint amongst club golfers is that their practice grounds are in poor condition. Unfortunately, this is often true, but all the same practice is beneficial to your golf game, and you really should make use of them.

Creating interest

The first priority is to avoid boredom. You'll probably get the most enjoyment from doing the things you are already good at. There's nothing wrong with that. You can practise what you do well and get to do it even better. This is what a lot of golfers do – for example, whenever I see a rather poor golf swing in a low handicapper I'm apt to enquire – you might say brutally! – if the golfer in question is a short-game wizard. Often he or she has adopted the 'maximum enjoyment' approach to practice and achieved nearly professional standards at chipping and putting to the detriment of other parts of their game.

At the other extreme, there's the chap who exults in seeing his drives soar away and practises little else. Well, if you reach a standard where you're nearly always in play from the tee and a long way down the fairway, you've set yourself up to play the rest of the hole to perfection. At worst, you're unlikely to drop more than one shot.

On the other hand, you may never experience real difficulty in escaping from bunkers. But how close do you get the ball to the hole? You may well find it fun to develop true feel for this part of the game. Who knows, you may become your club's answer to Gary Player and hole out from time to time. After all, didn't the great man say: 'The more I practise the luckier I get'?

Even if you still don't break 80 every time you go out, there is quite a glow from excelling at any department of golf.

For me, however, one of the most satisfying

aspects of practising is to fly the irons at the flag. For this, a practice green, even if not strictly essential, is much more fun than hitting into a flat, featureless field. If your club doesn't have one, I can only suggest that you campaign for one. Although there may not be room for a full-scale practice ground, this facility is not very demanding on space and the greens staff can make it a winter job.

Once you have established that practice needn't be boring you shouldn't stop short at this, but should try to raise your overall standards at all kinds of shot-making.

This also needn't be boring either, provided that you have the right approach. I see many golfers, and not a few tournament players amongst them, apparently happy to take out a hundred or so balls. They'll hit them off, sometimes two or three in the air at once, fetch them, and then on with the same routine. This is asking for trouble. It's just exercise really.

I suggest just 20 or 30 balls would do just as well, together with a more thoughtful approach. Don't just swing away with one club after the other but think out what you're trying to achieve with every shot. If you've a 5 iron in your hand, for instance, try to hit them both high and low, and you'll really be a golfer if you can also swing them in to a target from both left and right. This kind of experimenting is far from boring.

Also vary the lies you give yourself. In order to build confidence, by all means start by nudging your ball into a nice lie. Then test yourself from less favourable places – a downslope, a fluffy lie, bare patches and divots. Put yourself in some horrid places in the rough. This is excellent for strengthening the hands, as used to be recommended by Gary Player, and it will teach you what results you can actually get while in play. See what happens when your ball is laying well down in wet grass, and which club can 'get a result'. How does the ball behave? You'll soon find that experience will show you after not many attempts from the edge of the practice ground. Where once you took a 5 or 6 iron you may well find that an 8 or 9 is all

your hand speed can really cope with. You may also learn how good a sand iron can be when you are aiming only to get your ball back to the fairway. When your ball is really buried, use it almost the same way as from sand. Hit perhaps a couple of inches behind the ball and keep the clubhead moving through the ball. Your clubface may not actually meet the ball but the 'explosion' will force the ball up and out as long as you have only twenty yards or so to go.

Especially after a long lay-off, don't practise for too long, but instead try to practise often. Perhaps the ideal is half an hour, followed by playing a few holes, and finally another half hour. Depending on the amount of time you have, this kind of regime is much preferable to spending two or three hours on the practice ground and then shunning it for the rest of the season because you found it boring. Frequent practice for short periods is more beneficial than rare long bursts.

Of course, it's fetching the balls that's half the trouble, isn't it? This is not so if you go to a driving range. (How I wish they called them 'practice ranges'. Using the word 'driving' seems to result in a high proportion of golfers doing just that and nothing else.) Unfortunately, the solid balls on offer at most ranges leave a lot to be desired, so you cannot expect the ball to fly as far as it should.

Whatever and wherever you're practising, however, things will so often go much better after a lesson. As an experienced golfer, you probably think of seeking your professional's advice only when going through the doldrums, and see him as the doctor you want to cure what ails you. But he may be able to suggest a small adjustment that will immediately knock a shot or two from your handicap. If you don't want to go to him, find out if there's a another good teacher nearby.

Lessons

Lessons are not just for when things are going badly; in fact, you may get more real benefit when playing quite well. Seve Ballesteros told how in 1984 he had been on good form, but had developed a minor swing fault. Jaime Gonzalez of

Brazil and the Argentine Vicente Fernandez made some suggestions while they were out on the practice round at St Andrews and, of course, Seve went on to win the Open.

Oddly the vast majority of golfers seek advice only for the full golf swing. It's very rare to hear a club golfer ask for a lesson in, say, putting or chipping. But with these quite slow-motion shots, a basic fault of technique shows up very obviously,

and an instant 'cure' is really far more likely than when you're swinging at more or less full power. The trouble is that most golfers think that it's just nerves that make them have a poor short game, but while nerves certainly come into it, so does technique. Before the 1980 season and after his worst year ever Jack Nicklaus took lessons on the short game from Phil Rodgers as he didn't have sufficient range of shots at his command from

Practise the unusual, such as a plugged ball in a bunker (but repair the damage to the bunker afterwards!).

Warming up exercises.

close to the green. The result proved that he wasn't 'finished' and he won two major championships. If he can think that way, why not you?

Occasional lessons and advice are essential adjuncts to practice, or else you may find that you are practising the same fault over and over again.

WARMING-UP

This is not really practice at all and means what it says. It just isn't sensible to rush to the 1st tee, have a couple of quick swishes at a dandelion and think you are ready to take your first hit of the day.

No tournament professional behaves like this unless he's been caught in a traffic jam or slept in.

Before picking up a club coax the muscles and joints loose in the following way:

1 Make a short series of shoulder turns, just as you would in the golf swing. Begin gently and work up to a fuller turn than in your own swing.

2 Twist from side to side from the waist, allowing

your arms to hang limp and just follow the body movement. Do this rhythmically and without any sense of strain.

3 Do a few 'knees bends' to get the legs to feel lively. No need to go the full way down. About halfway is actually better and enough to make you feel you are wakening up the thigh muscles.

4 You are now ready to put all this into the context of the golf swing – but still without a club. Clasp your hands and swing to and fro, still gently and rhythmically.

So far, so good, and all it will take is a maximum of a couple of minutes. At the end of this little regime you should feel loose and also have reminded your muscles of the feel and rhythm of the golf swing.

You should now be ready to add a few clubs and not much more than a dozen balls. (This is a brief warm-up, as I said, *not* a practice session.) Select a short iron, say a wedge or a 9, and hit four or five shots. Next, move up to a mid-iron and repeat. All through, don't hit full out. Just try to carry through the feeling from our exercises of rhythm, gentleness and balance. You may be surprised that the ball goes rather further than you expect!

Top it all off, if you wish, with a couple of drives or fairway woods.

Off now to the practice green (if your club has one) for a few bunker shots and a chip or two, finishing off on the putting green.

Here, it's confidence and feel that should be your main aim. First, from close range, give yourself the morale booster of seeing the ball disappear into the hole. Do this from as close as you like, no more than eighteen inches. It's quite important not to miss any of these! Finally a few long putts. No need here to aim at the hole – you should be thinking and feeling the pace of the putting stroke. Only a few putts – I'm not in favour, immediately before a round, of too much time spent on the putting green, especially if it's not the same pace as those out on the course.

You may still not play the round of a lifetime but you've given yourself a chance, and you will feel ready to play.

FITNESS

So far, I've said little about physical fitness. When I was a young player most people felt that strong fingers and legs that could propel you comfortably about the course for 36 holes were just about all you needed.

There was the odd exception. Henry Cotton, a pundit for well over fifty years, always stressed that you must develop strength in the fingers, and recommended carrying a hard rubber ball in the pocket and squeezing it in every idle moment. He also preached the usefulness of 'hitting and stopping', by which he meant preventing the follow-through after a shot, so as to put stress on the muscles of the fingers, hands and wrists. Later, Henry became perhaps more extreme in his views, and had many disciples developing their hand and arm strength by hitting old car tyres. This is good but it's severe as well. You should

definitely start off rather gently.

Dai Rees, in his very different way, went further. He believed in total physical fitness and used to put many of us to shame by training at Highbury with the Arsenal football team.

Even today, only a few major players have found that sheer exercise much improved their games. Jack Nicklaus, for instance, believes that taking part in other sports is helpful, particularly as it may freshen the mind on return to golf. In Britain, Sandy Lyle and Nick Faldo are amongst those who believe in the value of jogging, and Arnold Palmer has certainly been photographed taking an early morning run.

However, the general belief of the past still holds sway, that the best fitness training for golf is playing the game. By playing a lot you develop the muscular strength and suppleness you need.

There is a lot of truth in this. The key to a good golf game is first and foremost rhythm and balance, and there's no magic formula in the way of exercise. There have been players who have actually lost their games after heroically losing a lot of weight. The sudden change has disturbed both the rhythm and balance, although certainly reducing their weight *gradually* would have been beneficial.

However, we do have an extreme example of a man who believes fitness is vital to good golf. That man, of course, is Gary Player. He has taken a lot of exercise, abstained from alcohol, tea and coffee and preached the value of a balanced, simple diet. He trains with weights and has done so for many years. A small man, he has tried to make up for lack of height and weight by greater muscle strength, primarily so that he could get up at the par 5s in two.

So exercise cannot be ruled out as being of no help; you have to look at what would suit your own game and ambitions best. If you are soon out of breath on a mild upslope, or tire towards the end of a game, or always avoid playing 36 holes, then you are just not golf fit. Exercise may be the answer, or reducing your intake of both food and alcohol.

CLUBMANSHIP

Enormous sums of money are spent on equipment every year, and a lot of it is wasted. The player is seduced by the quiet glow of new woods or the glitter of irons. A waggle or two, perhaps even a full swing, and they are for him.

This is just not the way to go about buying the tools of your golfing trade. It is feel and performance, not appearance, that count. Be particularly careful not to be entranced by a club because it is the latest style, or because one of your friends swears by it. Golf is an individual game, and what works for someone else will not necessarily work for you. When you see some clubs that you like, seek advice about them, look at them hard, and try them out.

When you find yourself drawn to those new clubs in the shop, ask the professional for his advice. Get him to look your swing over. Then be prepared to wait a little. It's possible those seductive clubs don't really suit you. Perhaps the lies are too flat or too upright. You might be better off with slightly longer or shorter shafts, a higher or lower swing weight. What about the flex of the shafts? They could be too whippy or too stiff. Is that flex in the right place for your type of play? Some players are best suited with the flex to-wards the grip, others with it nearer the clubhead.

Check out the grips. Some are manufactured with a raised line running from the butt to the bottom. It's there to help you by fitting into the fingers in a way that makes sure your clubhead is automatically square to the ball. Alas, that help is far more often a hindrance, as some grips are fitted very approximately indeed. You may seem to get some cut on the 6 iron while the 4 is apt to give you a hook, because the bad alignment of the grip may cause you to shut the face of the 4 and

The raised line along the grip helps you hold the club in such a way that the clubhead is square to the ball.

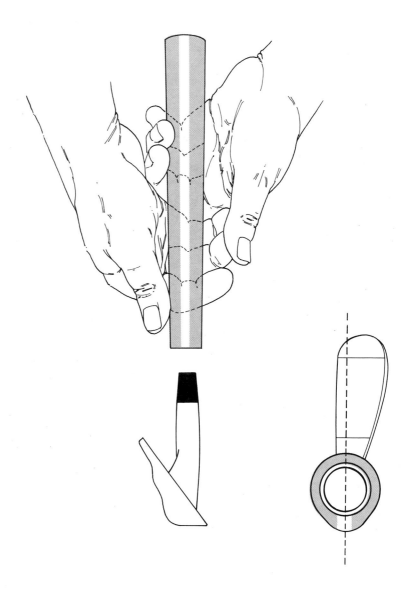

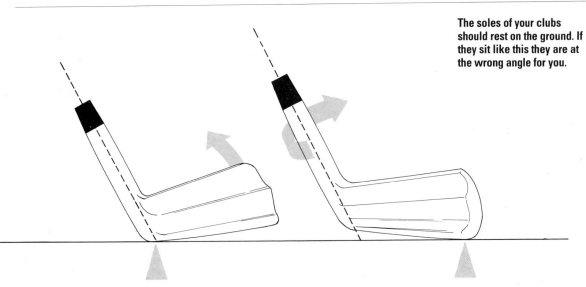

The soles of your clubs should rest on the ground. If they sit like this they are at the wrong angle for you.

open up the 6. Reject such clubs without hesitating.

You should also ask your professional to check each club for loft and lie. It's amazing, despite modern manufacturing techniques, how, say, a 7 iron may have the same loft as an 8. In effect, you'll be carrying around a club that's of very little use. Both will hit the ball, from a perfect swing, almost the same distance when you've a right to expect a difference of around ten to fifteen yards between them.

Even more disastrous are the lies. They could make you swing too steep or too flat or catch the ground with toe or heel.

Although your professional's advice ought to be invaluable, in the end you're the one who is going to use the clubs and your investment is considerable, so insist on trying them out. This doesn't mean you will scratch them as they can be taped for protection and you can also play them off a mat. Your professional may also have a few clubs set aside for demonstration.

Try them out on the practice ground, and not just on one sunny day but at least two. One's feel for a club can differ so much from one day to the next.

These are just a few general points but I think they're ones that so many golfers totally fail to consider. Let's go on to cases.

LIGHTWEIGHT CLUBS

Lightweight clubs are a development that is worth investigation by all golfers. Perhaps to oversimplify the theory, the basic idea is that a club decelerates as it approaches impact. A light-

The theory of lightweight clubs is that they get through the ball quicker.

173

weight one does so less than a conventional one. It is claimed that a normal club begins decelerating when parallel with the ground at about hip height, but that lightweights slow down much later, producing some 5 per cent extra distance.

It has been argued for some twenty years that there is an ideal weight of driver to suit each particular player. Broadly speaking, it is the one he can swing the fastest in relation to its mass. A slow swinger may well benefit from rather a heavy club while a fast swinger could be using a club that's too heavy for him to get the full benefit from his speed through the impact area. So far, so good, but I feel much less confident in recommending similar benefits for irons, where the aim should be accuracy. When hitting and holding a green, it doesn't matter much, if at all, what the number on the club is. Precision is the name of the game.

However, lightweight clubs have been vastly successful in America since 1983 and were selling like hot cakes in Britain the following year in various areas.

They weigh about 1½ ounces less than their conventional equivalents and have a swingweight of around C/4 instead of the average D/0 to D/3.

Personally I have always preferred heavy clubs because they enable me to feel the head throughout the swing. To me, that is of paramount importance, and such feel is diminished for most players if very light clubs are used.

However, a very light shaft weight is always beneficial. If that condition is met, the heads can be proportionally lighter, provided that one can feel the clubhead whatever the weight of the club as a whole.

I advise you not to jump in cheque book first (the clubs are rather expensive) but to try them out on your practice ground to see if they do work for you.

METAL WOODS

I've said it before and I'll say it again, but 'metal woods' is perhaps the silliest expression in all the language of golf, but they do seem to be here to stay, although traditionalists like me are rather wary of them. Although many club golfers buy drivers first, I think the fairway woods are rather more worth a try, as their feel is very good. Some professionals now use a metal 3 from the tee and drop the driver from the bag, as they find it has a safer loft and still gives good distance, while some others find it gives them more distance from a normal fairway lie. Like Mr Ping's 1 iron, the fairway clubs will live on, especially if they are designed for specific shots, like the baffy of old, the Ginty or just a conventional 5 wood. Perhaps

Right: A metal wood *right* has a larger sweet spot than an ordinary wood, which allows for a greater margin of error in striking the ball.

Far right: A laminate driver *top;* persimmon (*middle*); and metal wood.

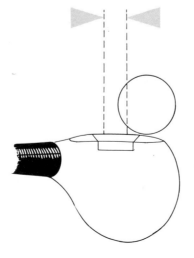
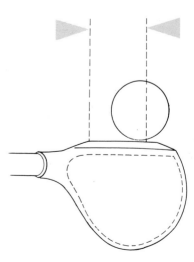

Cross-section of a metal wood

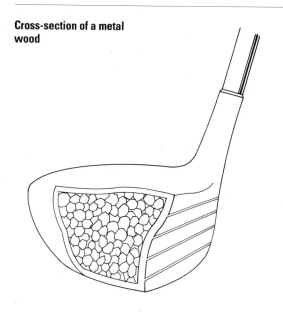

At the most lofted end of the range, many players have found a 7 is a very good substitute for the long irons. It's especially good for dealing with a tight lie and a ball quite well down in the rough. But beware, these clubs do sometimes fly the ball much further than you expect, leaving you well through the green, perhaps.

Any metal club has one minor advantage well worth having. If you break one, you can be sure that the replacement will be exactly the same weight and shape.

PERSIMMON AND LAMINATES

To many club golfers a wood is just a wood. If their clubs have a black or any dark finish I doubt they are aware if they have persimmon heads or maple laminates. Actually, I think it's a crime to conceal what may be a fine wood, and also an opaque finish on a persimmon club may have an ulterior purpose. It hides the grain pattern, and this can be quite important, for while some companies will reject wood that is unsatisfactory, others will happily use it for their most expensive clubs.

Ideally, as you look down at the clubhead, the centre of the grain whorl should be near the toe. The U shape of the grain means that the head is less likely to suffer if damp gets in. This pattern may not affect the length of drive but it will the life of the club.

Closeness of grain is also important. Almost all persimmon comes from the Southern States of the USA and grows on ground that is wet, often flooded by rivers in the spring. Ideally, the original block from which the club is made should be heavy, as drilling out to add lead, as is common with the lighter woods, inevitably must weaken the strength of the head. Well, I'm afraid you can't ask if the particular batch you look at came from Kentucky because you are highly unlikely to get any answer at all, yet this is probably the ideal area. The wood will have grown slowly and in consequence will be close-grained. The other persimmon areas in the USA such as Louisiana and Florida have hotter climates, and as a result

even, instead of 'metal wood', the old names will return, and once more we'll be pulling a brassie, spoon or baffy out of the bag.

With drivers, many professionals believe that the solid ball, especially, flies off the clubface faster than anything seen before. That speed, of course, means more distance. Other people, however, find they hit the ball less far, but straighter. The problem with them is that there is far less feel, and have to see how far the ball goes before they can be sure how well they hit it.

Their main advantage is that a shot struck not 100 per cent does still travel quite well in average summer conditions. This is because, as with heel-and-toe weighted putters and irons, the sweet spot is larger. The off-centre shot still goes well enough.

The invention of John Zebelean, an aerospace metallurgist and designer, they have a hollow interior filled with polyurethene foam to lessen the ringing sound of ball against clubhead. The outer skin is thickened to increase weight. This, of course, is done with the fairway clubs. Prices have come down considerably since these clubs first came out but it's well worth trying one out before making an investment.

Persimmon

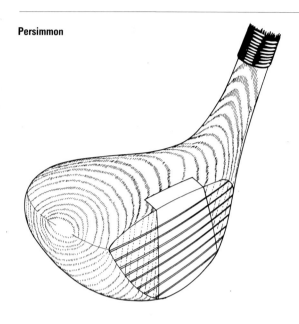

growth is faster and the grain wider. The wood is therefore lighter. Though not ideal, because it must be more lead-weighted, the eventual result may well be fully satisfactory, as long as the basic grain-pattern guidelines I've mentioned have been followed.

By now, you may well be wondering if, really, it wouldn't be far simpler to give persimmon a miss. Isn't it more trouble than it's worth? In fact, I haven't been talking about trouble but about what you should look out for, and what you should try to avoid. Concert violinists cherish a Stadivarius. A good persimmon head is in that class to a golfer. Some people, for instance, think that clubhead design of woods (Tommy Armour's or MacGregor's, for example) reached a kind of peak during the 1950s and 1960s and will part with considerable sums of money to buy certain models of the period. It's only the heads they are after, for current shafts and grips are much better.

At the end of the day, it's really a matter of what club you are comfortable with, or in the case of a top-class persimmon head, proud of. If you are confident with the club, and think you will hit it better, then that is far more likely to be the result. Speaking as a former tournament professional, and knowing intimately so many from past and present, I know that confidence is the first essential, though love can come into it, too – I've still got a favourite few tucked away.

Maple laminates

The average maple laminate head is far more likely to be satisfactory than a poor persimmon. For a start, if you seldom (perhaps never) protect your wooden clubs, at least the layers of maple laminate and present-day adhesives are likely to be effective against damp, provided that the polyurethane surface is unblemished. Apart from the basic feel of the clubhead, and how it conforms to the groove of your own particular swing, it is less likely to crack than persimmon. The glue helps. There are two things to look at in a laminated clubhead. The grain should travel down the neck in a shaft-to-head direction – I think you'll find it always does – and the 'rose' or position of the central whorl of the laminates at the centre of the pattern as you look down at the clubhead should be fairly central. This greatly affects the feeling of the player, as to whether or not the clubface is open, shut or square.

The whorl in this maple laminate is very pronounced.

177

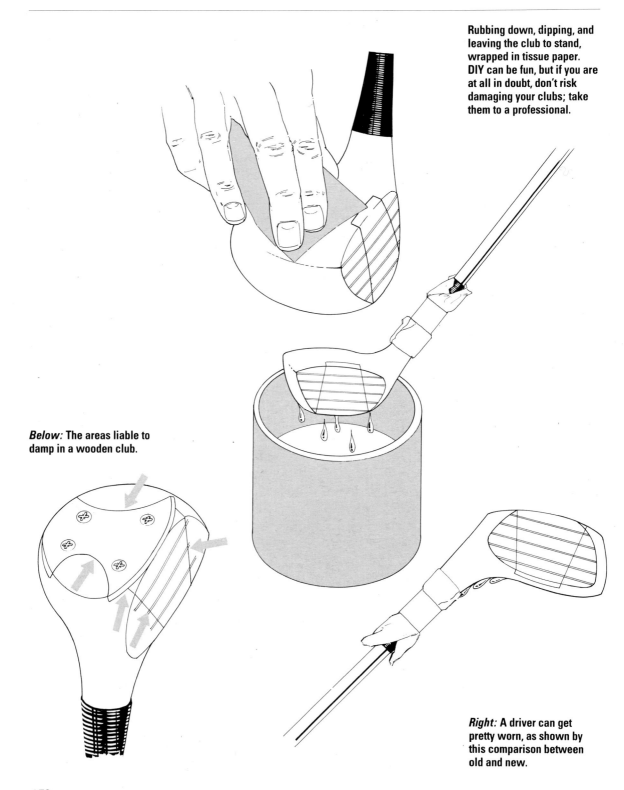

Rubbing down, dipping, and leaving the club to stand, wrapped in tissue paper. DIY can be fun, but if you are at all in doubt, don't risk damaging your clubs; take them to a professional.

Below: The areas liable to damp in a wooden club.

Right: A driver can get pretty worn, as shown by this comparison between old and new.

WOOD MAINTENANCE

Damp is the enemy of wood, and must be kept at bay. The danger areas are at the edges of the inserts and the join of the sole plate with the club sole. Inevitably, with impact shock, there is movement between either face and head or soleplate and head, and it will eventually break the polyurethane seal. Damp can then seep in.

Check regularly to see if this has happened. If it has, there is a very temporary remedy which will keep your clubhead in good condition: polishing with a quality wax or a standard car polish. Simply clean the clubhead with a damp cloth, dry it, and then apply the polish, making sure to get it into the cracks in the polyurethane finish around face insert and soleplace.

If the surface has deteriorated too far, it really is not very difficult to totally re-finish the club. It just needs patience and care to achieve good results. Because this is a labour-intensive job, your professional will charge a decent fee as re-finishing just one club takes a long time – say six to a dozen hours spread over several days. Some professionals are superb craftsmen, and you may well be able to find one in your area. If not, it's possible to tackle the job yourself, providing that you realize it's not a quick job.

If deterioration of the finish has not gone far, buy a pot of polyurethane clear varnish and thin it down. Clean and dry the head and rub it down all over with a very fine wire wool or abrasive paper. Then dip it in the varnish as far as the whipping. Wrap some tissue paper around the bottom of the whipping so that excess varnish will be absorbed when you stand the club up to cure, grip downwards so that the varnish runs towards the heel, not the toe.

Leave the club in a dust-free room (avoid one where people are passing to and fro). When the varnish is dry, rub down gently with the wire wool, or abrasive paper, aiming just to remove any high spots. Repeat the dip, following the same procedure. You must then contain your impatience to rush out onto the course with your gleaming new club. Wait at least five days, and preferably ten, by which time the new surface will have cured to maximum hardness.

However, if the deterioration is well advanced you must strip the head down completely. Here a vice is valuable, though you may be able to get by without one. Remove the sole plate, though it can

Removing the sole plate

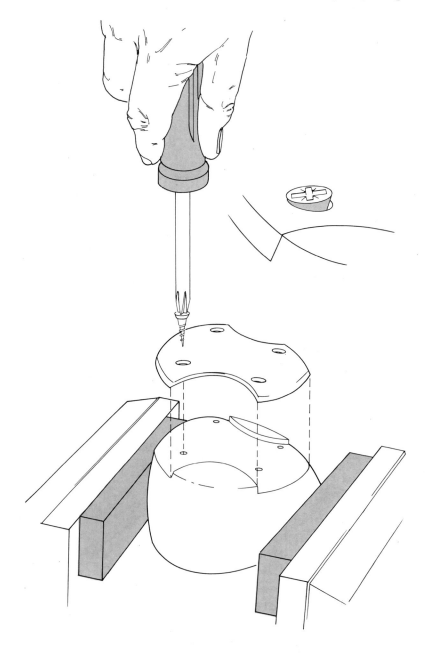

be left in place if it fits flush. The heads of brass screws are soft and very easily damaged, so make sure you use the right kind of screwdriver. It is easy to make them impossible to remove in a twinkling of an eye and you then have to drill them out – no easy task and one that requires precision equipment. If you pass this test of your skill satisfactorily, don't just toss the screws into a box. Each must eventually go back into the same hole, so draw the outline of the sole and insert of your club roughly on a piece of card and pierce the card with each screw as you remove it. If you do not do this, you will find that the screws do not fit flush and that, for example one or more screw edges are proud of the surface. They would then have to be filed and sanded flush and some of the screwhead would be lost, making it unlikely that a screwdriver could ever remove it again. Unless you are very confident, leave the insert well alone. Problems are all too likely.

It is necessary to remove the whipping to achieve a result of the highest standard.

You are now ready to remove the paint or varnish finish. Apply a coat of any normal proprietory paint stripper, wash and get as much off as possible using a fairly blunt kitchen knife – blunt so

that you don't inadvertently cut into the wood itself. It's probably as well to apply the stripper three times, for any residue will very quickly clog your abrasive paper or wire wool, and make it useless. Never use a coarse grade. You may scratch the wood too deeply and your eventual finish will not be perfect. Once there is no trace of the original finish, move to progressively finer grades of paper, or wool.

When you are dealing with the clubface itself, it may be necessary to recut the grooves if these have been hammered and compressed flat by years of use. In this case, use a fine hacksaw blade after filing the sides flat. Sand smooth when you're satisfied.

Your sole plate is very likely to be chipped and scratched by repeated contact with the ground, especially in the case of fairway woods. The leading edge, in particular, is very likely to be scarred and dented. In this case, begin work with a fine file and move on to progressively finer grades of abrasive paper. Check how the fit with both sole and face of your club is working out. You may find it necessary to remove a little material from the sole of your wood if swelling has taken place, or, alternatively you may need to build it up

Recutting the grooves, first with a file or thin hacksaw blade and then with abrasive paper.

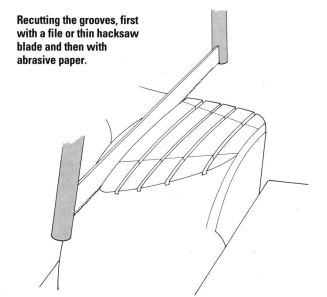

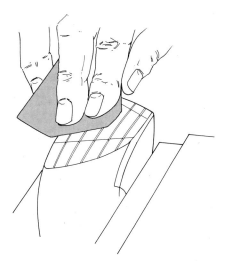

with epoxy resin if there has been any shrinkage.

When you are satisfied that you can do no more with head or soleplate, re-assemble them. Once the screws are well tightened, with a little epoxy resin in each hole, there will be a little final smoothing to ensure that all edges fit flush.

Many golfers will wish to get back to the original appearance of their club. This will seldom be quite possible if it had decals, giving the name of the manufacturer, model or contracted player, for example. However, this information is often applied by stamping followed by paint. If so, you can apply the same colour of paint to the impression and then remove the surplus. Do this after the first varnish dip.

When the paint is dry, you are ready to proceed with the dipping process that will lead to the final excellent finish – and many more years of club life.

Do not be in too great a hurry at this stage. The more coats you apply, the tougher, and more pleasing, the eventual result will be. Perhaps as many as six dips is ideal. Remember, finally, to allow the finish time to cure. You may prefer to ask the pro to do all this.

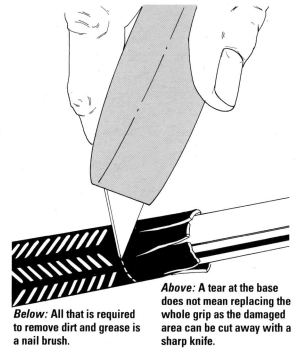

Above: A tear at the base does not mean replacing the whole grip as the damaged area can be cut away with a sharp knife.

Below: All that is required to remove dirt and grease is a nail brush.

RE-GRIPPING YOUR CLUBS

Assuming, like most of us, you have composition grips on your clubs, you can easily keep them in good order for a few years. The first part of a composition grip to suffer is usually the bottom of the taper. As the club is pushed into the bag, the edge knocks and catches against other clubs and the divisions in the bag. Sooner or later a tear will open. This need not be the end of that particular grip. Just get out a sharp knife or a razor blade and cut round the circumference. Make sure you remove all of the tear. As grips almost always extend further down the shaft than is strictly necessary, the half inch removed will do no harm. Indeed, you can probably repeat this process two or three times before the grip has to be discarded.

The grip as a whole always needs a little simple regular attention. However clean you may think they are, your hands will all the time be putting a

little grease and dirt on the grips. This is easily removed by a quick scrub with a nail brush and detergent, remembering to rinse thoroughly. But your hands will also be smoothing the surface of the grip imperceptibly.

At worst, when they are sweaty on a hot day, or in damp weather, it can be well-nigh impossible to hang onto the club. Much the same applies when hands and grips become wet in the rain.

This is the time to change the grip, though a gentle rub over with abrasive paper will keep it usable for a while. Some professionals can be quite fussy about the grade of abrasive paper they use because it can affect the feel of the grip. Most of them prefer to use a fine paper, mainly because so little of the composition surface is actually lost, but others feel that a rough abrasive gives a 'softer' feel.

Eventually all grips wear out, some surprisingly quickly. They are very easy to remove. Cut up the shaft towards the butt and then tear the grip off. Remove the adhesive tape that remains, before roughening the shaft with abrasive, which

My own set includes several old favourites.

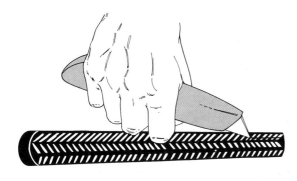

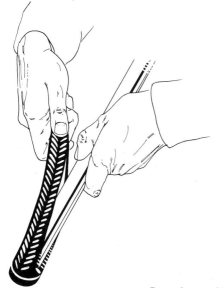

Removing an old grip.

This, he believes, means reduced grip pressure on the actual club.

I believe there are advantages in the relatively thick butt but that the bottom hand, where the grip is in the fingers, is best suited by a thickness that fits snugly. After all, this is the basic reason why all conventional grips taper from butt downwards.

If you want a thicker grip it can be achieved in either of two ways or by a combination of the two. The standard length of a grip when fitted is 10½ inches, longer, as we've seen, than strictly necessary. If you fit a grip not fully stretched it will, of course, be thicker. The effect, however, will mainly be felt lower down, where your bottom hand grips the club. The alternative method, to apply an extra ration of the adhesive tape applied according to your own preference, is a more certain way of thickening exactly where you want it.

These matters decided, we are ready to get down to the final stage. Moisten your tape well with solvent to make the adhesive soluble temporarily and slide the grip on, working it away from the butt. Don't stretch the lower section of the grip only, a common mistake. Allow one or two days for the adhesive to set.

The shaft should be firmly held in a vice. It is possible to do without one, perhaps bracing the clubhead against your foot, but it does make the whole job more difficult. It also leads to some loss of precision. And precision is required because most of the grips I know of have a guide ridge. This must be aligned 'under' the shaft so that it's parallel with the leading edge of your clubhead, in which case unless, you like to play with your clubhead toed in or slightly laid off, make adjustments accordingly.

If you take care over this and achieve a uniform result, you will have beaten some of the manufacturers. Grips are all too often fitted in such a sloppy manner that we golfers would be better off without a grip line. If you don't believe me, line up your own clubs and check. If you set the grip line at right angles to the target line I'm afraid you'll

helps the new tape to adhere better.

Of course, you will have your replacements to hand! These can readily be obtained from specialist suppliers whose advertisements can be found in the golf magazines. They usually offer a choice of products and also supply double-sided tape and the simple fitting instructions.

Before getting down to the job, decide on how thick you like your grips to be. Gene Sarazen, for instance, had his built up to a remarkable extent, because he had small hands and felt it was easier to hold on to a thick grip. Jack Nicklaus prefers thickness also, but only at the butt end. He likes to feel that none of the last three fingers of his left hand will meet the fleshy pad below his thumb.

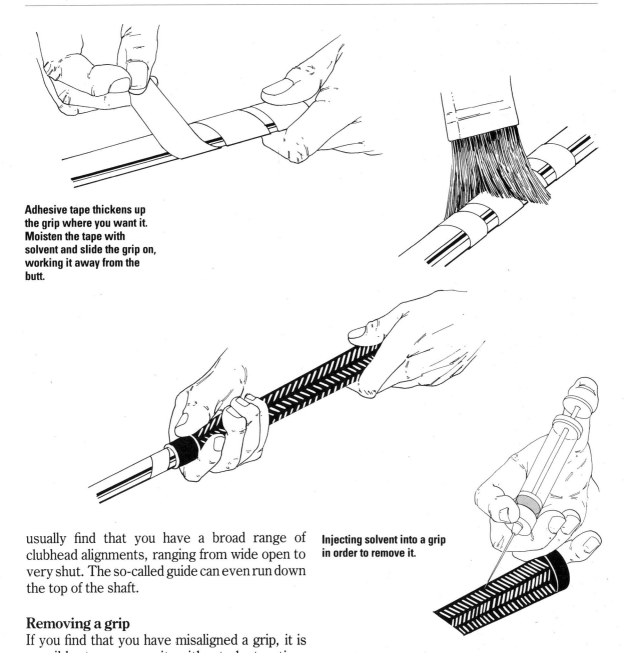

Adhesive tape thickens up the grip where you want it. Moisten the tape with solvent and slide the grip on, working it away from the butt.

Injecting solvent into a grip in order to remove it.

usually find that you have a broad range of clubhead alignments, ranging from wide open to very shut. The so-called guide can even run down the top of the shaft.

Removing a grip

If you find that you have misaligned a grip, it is possible to remove it without destruction. However, you will need a hypodermic syringe and you will face raised eybrows at the least if you attempt to purchase one at your local chemist, (drug store). If your quest is successful, however, fill it with solvent and inject through the skin to the adhesive tape below. Do this freely.

It usually works and is well worth a try. You might also want to do this job if you break a shaft on a fairly new set of clubs and wish to maintain matching grips of identical feel.

All this can be fun but if at all in doubt go to your professional for help and service.

IN HARD TIMES

No one has ever played a perfect round of golf, in fact, such a thing is unattainable. There's a story about Ben Hogan which illustrates this well. In a dream, he scored holes-in-one all the way round (including all the par 5s!) except for one hole where, alas, he got down in 2. He awoke furious at that one lapse.

All golfers get into trouble, either on the course or with a fault, probably a technical one which is poisoning their whole game.

If you are plagued by, say, a fit of shanking, or are losing 40 per cent of your distance, as I once did for a spell, because of a choppy, cutting attack on the ball, it really is time to pause for thought and to work the problems out on the practice ground.

Here are some thoughts on how to set about it.

CURING THE SHANK

This is a taboo subject in some professional circles – after all, it can be an infectious disease. However, I feel fairly safe in discussing it, as I've hit only three in my life. Two of them were easily excused: I was bunkered in each case and playing from steep downhill lies. I think I probably got my hands too far in front of the clubhead and the face too open.

The other one was inexplicable. I was feeling that all was well with the world and was confronted with a 7 iron shot from a good lie in mid-fairway. Being my first real shank it didn't disturb me unduly, and fortunately it was also my last. My father Percy, one of our best British

This sad illustration shows one of my few shanks.

professionals in the 1920s and 1930s, claimed never to have had a single one. Dai Rees, however, was always liable to produce the occasional one; in his case it was the result of a loose grip at the top of the backswing. He shanked perhaps half-a-dozen times a year and one of them probably cost him an Open Championship – with a 6 iron at that, which is quite unusual for a pro.

The best thing to do after such occasional shanks is to dismiss them from your mind. Tell yourself you must have made a horrific swing.

It's another matter if the disease persists. I remember long ago giving a sufferer a lesson at Parkstone Golf Club. He shanked every shot with short irons, even to the extent of twice circumnavigating a green! I found a solution in the end but after that first lesson there'd been no progress so we retired to the clubhouse for very large brandies and sodas. He was actually in tears. So was I!

As there is no one cause of a shank, I'll deal with all the causes one by one, and also how to bring about a cure. In most cases, it is obvious if you can isolate the cause.

1 In-to-out swing path. The more a player has this movement, the more likely he is to become an occasional shanker or socketer of the ball. It stands to reason, with this approach into the ball, that shots not hit out of the middle of the clubface will always fall towards the socket. The opposite is also true: you seldom meet a consistent slicer hitting more than the occasional socket. His errors are more towards the toe of the club as he draws the clubhead in towards his body.

The tendency of the 'in-to-out' player to shank always seems to be increased if he has a flat swing. The cure is none too easy: have a less strong in-to-out approach to the ball and try to swing more upright. I also suggest that you have a strong mental image of the *middle* of your clubface meeting the middle of the ball. Don't be content, at least while suffering from shanking, just to swing the clubhead through the ball.

2 The hurried shot. If you swing back jerkily and fast and, naturally, follow the same pattern on the downswing, you are likely to throw your clubhead

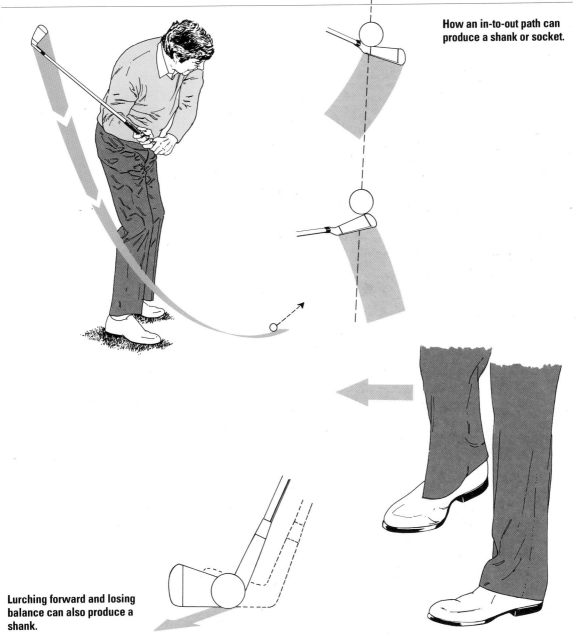

How an in-to-out path can produce a shank or socket.

Lurching forward and losing balance can also produce a shank.

off path. This can result in either a socket or a toe hit. Swing more easily and rhythmically.

3 Forcing the shot. This has the same result as **2** and the same cure: rhythm, balance and timing.

4 Lack of wrist action. Here the player will subconsciously feel that he's not putting enough into the shot and try to compensate with a lunge of shoulders and body.

5 Falling forward. At least among poor players this may well be the most common cause of shanking. Off balance, the player lurches towards the ball. Of course, anything can happen then.

6 Weight on toes. This will produce the same result as **5**. The cure is to set your weight towards the heels, exaggerating this for a while, though you will want to get back to the balls of the feet as soon as possible.

7 Standing too close. Players sometimes go through a phase, perhaps in trying to cure some other fault that has crept into their game, of moving nearer the ball. When this position becomes excessive, there isn't any room to swing. When the ball is really close, it's almost impossible not to shank.

8 Standing too far from the ball. Of course, this is the reverse of **7**. This time there's room in plenty to swing, but in reaching out for the ball the player is likely to be off balance and lurch into the hitting area. The result may well be a shank.

These then are the main causes and the rather uncertain cures. If the disease persists, professional consultations become urgent, provided that your pro is not afraid of catching the disease himself. However, I do have one message of good cheer. It's possible to go to bed a sufferer and wake up with the curse gone in the night. Who knows, perhaps for ever – but not unless you swing the clubhead with rhythm and balance.

As a generalization, be ready to forgive yourself for a shank in a bunker. Even the best of players are occasional perpetrators when the ball is awkwardly placed or the stance difficult and off-balance. You are also playing with an open clubface usually and this increases the likelihood of a shank by many percentage points.

HOOKING

When Bobby Locke emerged, he was good enough to win his own national championship, the South African Open, as an amateur, and also proved more than able to hold his own in Britain against the best professionals. But at this time (say 1934 to 1938) he cut nearly all his shots. It would certainly be unfair to call him a slicer, but he certainly played with fade.

Whereas the fade is the best pattern of flight for powerful players, Locke wasn't one of these. Encountering little run on the British fairways, he found that he was being outdriven far too often. But he knew that for him the swing had to be rhythmical, and balanced, with no feeling of physical force being applied in the hitting area. He decided he would have to learn to draw the ball to get length, perhaps twenty yards. In due course Locke turned himself into the only great player to *hook* – yes, hook as distinct from draw – so much so that certain sour American professionals insisted that he even hooked his putts!

In all this, Locke was a one-off. It's all very well to get an extra fifty yards on your tee shot, but that shape is a nightmare when playing short irons to hard greens. Locke was the only player I have ever seen who could achieve a high flight and a soft landing.

For the rest of golfing mankind, the controlled hook is fine for length down the fairway but is always inferior to the straight or faded shots when you're trying to hold the ball to a target. Some club golfers who draw every shot can only play effectively in the winter when the greens are at their most holding.

The basic cause of hooking is a shut clubface at the moment of impact. Depending on swing path, this can produce very variable results. If your path is in-to-out the right-handed player will see his ball start off right of target and swing back towards it. If the path is straight, the ball will start on target and then swing away left. If the path is from out-to-in, the ball will fly left, the amount depending on how closed the clubface is and how much you are swinging across the ball.

The last of these paths is no good at all. With it, you can only slice or pull the ball. The in-to-out path means that you'll *have* to play with a shut face. If you adjust, all that will happen is either a push to the right or slice. If your swing path is exaggeratedly in-to-out, you won't often remain on the golf course, unless you can somehow manage to hook it back.

The straight swing path is far more easy to deal with. In theory, all the golfer with a straight flight, followed by a sharp draw, has to do is adjust the position of the club in his hands. Though mechanical perfection is impossible, you should quite quickly reach a point where the flight is at least consistent.

Of course, there's more to curing the hook than this. Here are the other main causes and accompanying remedies.

1 A loose grip with the top hand will allow the bottom hand to whip through too fast in the hitting area. Make sure your top hand is firm through impact.

2 You may be standing with shoulders, hips and feet in a closed position. Stand square or a bit open to the target line.

3 If you play with the ball in mid-stance, this seems to encourage players to take the club away on the inside. Move it forward to just inside the front heel.

4 If your stance is too wide, this may have produced a big shoulder turn while your leg action is restricted.

5 If your legs fail to lead during the downswing, a free swing of the arms is prevented. Instead, you may get too much hand and wrist action leading to a closed clubface at impact.

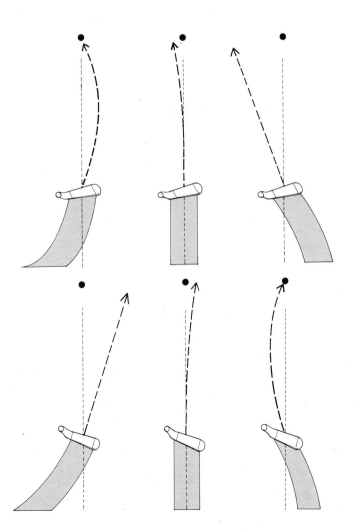

The basic cause of hooking is a shut face at impact. An in-to-out swing produces a ball that starts off right off target, then swings back towards it *top left;* a straight one, a ball that swings left *top centre;* and an out-to-in path one that flies to the left of the target *top right.* An open face is the cause of the slice. The same paths with an open face produce a ball that veers to the right of the target *bottom left;* that starts straight and then swings away to the right *bottom centre;* and that starts off target but curls back towards it *bottom right.*

6 If your grips are very thin, you may find this emphasizes the role of the fingers and a general wristiness. Try thicker grips. This will shift the emphasis to the hands and often results in better countrol of the clubface.

THE SLICE

I'm afraid the main reason why golfers slice is rather daunting. It's a natural action. The body wants to move in a way that causes a golf clubhead to cut across the ball.

Let's pause a moment, and consider the normal person taking a swat at a wasp. Do they stand nicely side on to the target with their rolled-up newspaper? No. The shoulders will be definitely open and the blow, for a right-hander, will swing distinctly from right to left. Positively no one will try to dispatch that troublesome insect with the newspaper on an in-to-out path.

Consider racket games – squash, tennis, badminton, racquets, fives, or table tennis. Most players feel more natural and hit with more power when the racket is travelling across the chest not away from or parallel with it – the cross court drive or volley in fact, rather than the shot down the line. This applies to either forehand or backhand.

Such players get away with this arc, even thrive and become champions and superstars. Alas, not the golfer. We must learn and keep a method which brings the clubhead in to the ball on a path to the target, while standing sideways on. To understand how to cure this cutting action, we have to look at what happens in a golf swing.

The power sources of the swing are hands and arms, turning the torso, and the leg action, each performing its role correctly. Hands and arms must swish into the impact point. If this movement is weak, the clubface will probably still be open at the decisive moment, and the more open the face, the greater the slice. The body turn must be a full one, enough to bring your back square to the target at the top of the backswing. Even a man like Doug Sanders, who only got the clubhead around shoulder high, still made a considerable shoulder turn. If you don't manage this, you'll inevitably start back to the ball with the clubhead still on the outside. The legs, on the other hand, provide little power in a good golf swing. What they should do is lead the downswing, both knees moving along the target line, followed by the natural turn of the shoulders and the full release of hands and arm.

Many poor golfers can manage a respectable backswing, but the whole thing then collapses as soon as the transition into the downswing begins. They often throw their hands and wrists from the top, and their shoulders then 'join in'. As a result they turn far too quickly, bringing the clubhead onto an out-to-in path. Disaster!

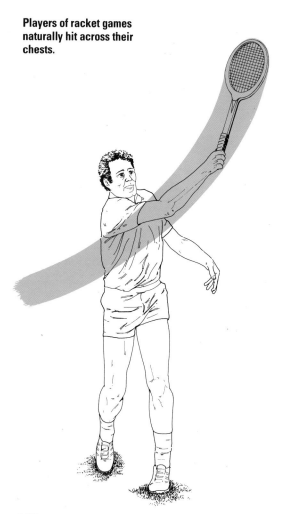

Players of racket games naturally hit across their chests.

On the other hand, there are those players who are far too 'shoulders dominated'. In everyday life, they make full use of them for anything that requires strength. This persists into their golf swing, and using them as the main power source of the swing results in that early movement down and across the ball and ineffective use of hands and arms. Remember always that only reasonable strength is needed in the golf swing: acceleration of a quite light implement and balance are the essentials. I'd back a ballet dancer to beat a caber tosser at golf any day of the week, if both started with reasonably good hand/eye coordination and ball sense. The first will know how to generate maximum power with the least effort, while the other will tend to rely on brute strength. Nevertheless, some players have a good swing path, but still slice, because, despite the good swing, their clubface is, again, open at impact.

You can tell if your swing path is on the target

The flight path of a slice. If you have tried everything and can't cure the fault, allow for the banana in aiming the shot.

line by noting the scars left by your divots. If they are straight, but your ball fades or slices, then this is what is happening (see p. 147).

In that case, first experiment with your grip. Could it be making it impossible to return your clubface anything but open? A right-handed golfer should turn *both* hands just a fraction to the right and get the shaft into the bottom of the fingers. Observe the result. It is possible to make the adjustment with either hand separately but I advise you not to do this. If your hands were correctly related to each other in the first place, you will have turned a plus into a minus. A basically sound grip could well become a poor one.

Persist with your adjustments to the grip until the ball begins to fly with at least a hint of draw. There's nothing that so delights and raises the confidence of a slicer as much as seeing his shots curve gently in the reverse direction!

If you can establish this pattern, you can gradually move back, if you wish, to hitting with fade, once the fear of slicing is well and truly behind you.

However, few people slice because of the position of their hands on the grip. A poor swing path is far more likely to be the cause.

You may have noticed that I've said nothing at all about alignment of the body with the target. This is as important as anything in golf, but I've seen a multitude of club golfers playing with very much a hooker's set-up who still contrive to slice every shot, because of these basic faults.

Two final points. If what you think of as a slice is simply a fade – your shots start off straight and don't start to bend until quite late in flight – rejoice! This is the safest kind of shot in golf and is used

These set-ups show in condensed form what happens when you slice or hook. In hooking *centre* the body ceases to be lined up with the target and in the backswing you turn your front shoulder to the target. In slicing *right* the front foot is set away from the target line, and at the top of the backswing the clubhead points off to the left of the target.

quite deliberately by a large majority of good tournament players.

If, on the other hand, you really have an awful slice, you may be able to play to your handicap and win your share of the money by being realistic and making full allowance for all those banana curves.

At bottom, however, you'll have little pride in your golf game. Far better to follow my advice, take a lesson, and get yourself on to the practice ground. Until the correct swing sequence becomes second nature, you'll find you have no real trust in it out on the course.

A poor downswing results in a quick turn and the clubhead approaches the ball on an out-to-in path.

Experiment with your grip: a poor one often keeps the clubface open at impact.

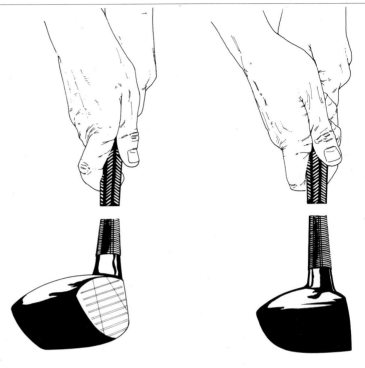

Trevino is an individualistic genius. Nearly every shot is played with fade. He keeps control with quite a strong grip.

LEARNING TO LIVE WITH THE TWITCH

The words 'twitch' and 'jerk' are mostly used in connection with putting. They describe that sad, and wounding, condition when a golfer is unable to make a smooth pass at the ball. It could be clearly seen in Bernhard Langer's putting in the two to four foot range during the 1982 and 1983 seasons. The little practice swings were impeccably relaxed and rhythmical but, for a while, you could lay odds that the West German would not be able to manage a smooth stroke when the dread time came actually to play the ball. A fatal tremor appeared and it looked pure chance if the ball dropped into the hole.

Before Langer became a major figure on the golf scene he had suffered the same affliction dreadfully, but corrected it for a while by the timely purchase of a lady's length Acushnet Bull's Eye putter, found in the back of Clive Clark's shop at Sunningdale Golf Club. In 1984 smoothness of stroke returned when he changed to a reversed hands putting grip, and he took the lead in the European Tour putting statistics. I have great admiration for Bernhard's superb abilities and hope the latest change to a ten-finger grip has done the trick. Certainly, he went on to win the 1985 US Masters, and seemed to have beaten the twitch for good – the only man I know to do so at this level of golf. Generally, however, in these matters I'm a pessimist. With Henry Longhurst, I believe that 'once you've had 'em, you've got 'em'.

Bobby Jones once described the condition. He said that as the putter came towards impact the ball 'seemed to disappear from sight'. For Harry Vardon it was the feeling that his right hand was about to jump. His solution was to take a quick stab at the ball before the jump happened – with, of course, deplorable results.

Other sufferers have included Ben Hogan, a most resolute holer-out into his forties. In the end, he used to stand like a pillar of stone, unable to move the putter as the seconds ticked agoni-zingly by. When he eventually succeeded, the result was a convulsive jerk, with no backswing and a flick follow-through. It was the main reason why he gave up competitive golf. If you are a sufferer, it can help to putt rather quickly. Don't allow time for the tension to build. Move to the ball, give quick glance along the line, and putt. If I had worked that one out before a certain US Masters, I probably wouldn't have taken ten putts from twelve feet! On another occasion, in Shell's *Wonderful World of Golf* in Bermuda, Jimmy Demaret remarked that I'd set back the cause of cross-handed putting by twenty-five years!

I remember partnering Gene Sarazen in an Open Championship early in my career. I felt that the American wasn't treating the event seriously. He'd just walk up to the ball, glancing along the line, and hit it almost before he'd come to a stop. There was absolutely no weighing-up of the texture of the green and its contours at all. Surely this was not the way to play during a major championship?

But, looking back, I'm sure Sarazen was trying to get the problem of putting out of the way before he became incapable, through tension, of making a smooth pass at the ball.

The other solution is to follow Langer's example and try different putters and grips. I relied on this myself, and several other professionals believe in it. It worked for Sam Snead in the early years after World War II, until alas, an assistant broke Snead's shaft and he was back to square one.

Another idea is to change your method drastically. The trouble seems to stem from the part of your body that's been at the centre of your own putting stroke. Be different. So, if you've always had the feeling that you are mainly using your forearms in the stroke, change perhaps to a wristy rap or *vice versa*. Alternatively, it might work for you if you set the emphasis on a stiff-armed action or the shoulder movement of a Bob

Right: Bernhard Langer is one of the few top players who has beaten the twitch and gone on to win major championships.

Charles, who, incidentally, suffers from the disease on occasion.

Non-putting twitches
For club golfers, the twitch may not appear at its worst in putting. Bunker play, even when technique looks adequate, can be a problem. Just as professionals have a memory store of all the putts that they ought to have holed, the club golfer may recall the many times he's thinned a bunker shot and seen his ball scuttle far through the green. To compensate, he may then have become far too tentative and weak with his stroke, the arms like loose pyjama cords. His ball stays in the sand.

Here the stroke required is a reasonably full one and this should help you – in theory. If you're nervous in bunkers, you must practise. You must have confidence about what happens when your sand wedge enters the sand. Have a lesson. So many people play their bunker shots in a way that makes success impossible.

With chipping and the very short pitch – say from twenty to thirty yards, we are back in the same sort of territory as putting. Both the calculation and execution of the stroke may be perfect but the result highly disappointing. Your ball catches a soft or hard spot and finishes yards away from where you had a right to expect. As in putting, extremely exact striking is vital but, alas, rather more difficult to achieve. My great friend David Thomas, a magnificent hitter, twice finished second in the British Open, on the first of these occasions, 1958, losing a 36-hole play-off to the great Australian Peter Thomson. Yet he was one of the worst chippers and short pitchers I've ever seen – at least amongst players of such class. In one *News of the World* Matchplay Championship at Turnberry he once putted round a bunker, and in the final against John MacDonald conceded one hole when faced with a little pitch over a bunker (he did, however, win the event).

David never got over his lack of confidence in these shots. Consequently, he was seldom able to score well unless his play through the green

was at top level. What an Achilles' heel to have!

Without these shots in his golfing armoury, how then did he prosper in tournaments? Well, as an immense and straight driver he could nearly always count on dominating the par 5s and on setting himself up well on the 4s. Nevertheless, he still missed his share of greens. He was then faced with those dreaded short shots up to the flag. He didn't have a twitch with the putter, so when there was no bunker or other hazard obstructing his route, he relied on this club as much as he could. They say that practice makes perfect, and certainly the more experience you gain of putting from off the green the more you are able to judge how your ball will run over the humps and hollows, through grass of different consistency, in the wet and in the dry. Thirty, even forty yards need not be too far.

So for sufferers with these shots, use your putter whenever you can. I know there seems to be a belief that this isn't a 'proper golf shot', but many of the great players have used the Texas wedge. Experience has taught them that what feels to be a good chip still doesn't finish as near the hole as just a fair putt from off the green.

Lastly we come to a condition for which there's no known cure: twitchiness with the driver. Amongst top professionals it's fairly rare. Even so, a very successful British professional of the early 1960's, the Midlander Ralph Moffit, caught the disease. In his case, he found it difficult to move the clubhead away from the ball. He was afraid of striking the ball and pulled back at impact, and eventually had to give up tournament golf.

A very good South African, Cobie Legrange, was also a sufferer. Despite winning the Dunlop Masters twice in the 1960s, he eventually confined his golf to his native land. He used to stop just after he had begun the take-away from the ball and a couple of other stutters occurred during his backswing.

Of course, this all happenened under the pressure of tournament play. Neither suffered in ordinary play. If it should happen to you under less stressful conditions there is an answer – but I'm

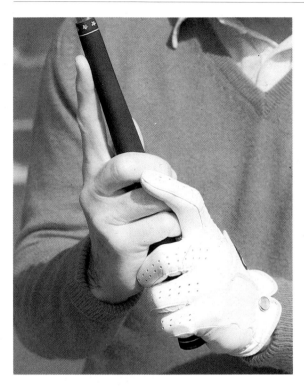

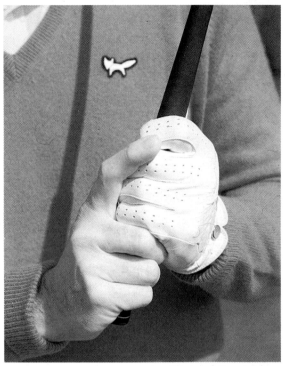

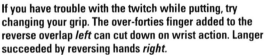

If you have trouble with the twitch while putting, try changing your grip. The over-forties finger added to the reverse overlap *left* can cut down on wrist action. Langer succeeded by reversing hands *right*.

afraid you have heard it before. You just have to take yourself off to the practice ground and work away until the rhythm of the golf swing feels the most natural thing in the world once more.

Lest you find what I have to say about 'the twitch' totally unbelievable or that sufferers must be ridiculously neurotic, let me assure you that it's scientific fact. Neurologists refer to the disorder as 'occupational cramps'.

Not only golfers suffer. The well-known condition, 'writer's cramp', was the first instance to be recognized. It can now be treated successfully by a small electric shock. Alas, an electrified golf club would inevitably be banned by the USGA and R & A, but perhaps a pocket device could be developed? Who knows?

It seems to be constant repetition that does it. Bank clerks counting money and farm workers milking by hand are amongst those subject to the disorder. Much more tragically, violinists are too. Imagine yourself in a packed Festival Hall or Carnegie Hall, bow poised. You can't move it or, perhaps worse, you suddenly lurch it across the strings, producing a screech. End of career.

Alas, I doubt if the violinist can drastically change his technique. For golfers, there is a possible message of hope: re-shape your swing. As I've said, this *is* possible in putting. You can switch from right-handed to left, spread hands wide, or use a reversed hands grip *à la* Bernhard Langer (employed by Alliss very successfully for a few years); indeed there are a few more possibilites, as I've outlined above.

You have my sympathy. I've suffered before and I fear I would again, especially if I had a downhill three-footer at St Andrews for the Open Championship. Under the pressure of competition we tend to revert to former styles. The same stance and grip are used once more. They worked very well once . . .

TAILPIECE

Now that you have reached the end of this book, I hope that you will have achieved my aim of knowing yourself and your game better. Once you have done that you have to decide how much you want to improve, and this will depend upon your ambitions in golf.

If you've found a new magic formula I'll be delighted, but that wasn't my real intention. Certainly there are mental tricks that might change your game overnight, but even then, you'll still have to work at it, to incorporate any change into your game so that it becomes instinctive. The new thought isn't likely to work for long, without some practice.

But have you the time? If it's difficult for you to get away for just a couple of games a week my bet is that you won't be willing to 'waste' that on the practice area even if it really will pay dividends in terms of the increased enjoyment you'll get from a higher standard of play. At least, try to make it a rule to arrive at your club a little early (after all it's getting home *late* that causes all the trouble, isn't it?) and hit a few balls on the practice area, puting something that you've learned from this book into effect. Do the same thing on the course, without preparation, and disastrous results are near certain. With one wrong move you'll abandon the new full swing thought or short game technique immediately and for ever – rather a waste of something that could work for you if you could manage to give

it the right kind of chance.

In the end, it's up to you. Golf is a game largely without coaches, managers and minders. It's for individuals and you walk alone. Decide what your ambitions are and what steps you are prepared to take to achieve them. Is it in your nature to be dedicated? Have you the time? Have you the talent?

The last of these will in some ways be hardest for you to answer. Golf, however, can be played quite well by almost anyone – if the work is put in and you learn to think well on the course.

If you decide that you don't really have enough talent, this isn't the time to give up. When the young Gary Player first came over to these islands in 1954, I was among those who thought he had no real feel for the game and advised him to give up the idea of making a career as a professional.

Player's superbly successful career makes nonsense of what I and others said. But Gary didn't become a golfer with great feel but made the most of other talents he possessed in high degree.

Go thou and do likewise!

The photographs on the following pages were
supplied by the sources indicated:
26 Bert Neale, 34 Michael Hobbs, 47 Michael
Hobbs, 53 BBC Hulton Picture Library, 57 Ken
Lewis, 58 Michael Hobbs, 62 Peter Dazeley, 63
Michael Hobbs, 74 (left) Ken Lewis, 77 Ken Lewis,
82 Peter Dazeley, 87 Peter Dazeley, 91 Michael
Hobbs, 93 Peter Dazeley, 103 Lawrence Levy, 113
Phil Sheldon, 117 Ken Lewis, 119 Phil Sheldon, 146
Michael Hobbs, 155 Peter Dazeley, 175 Michael
Hobbs, 199 Peter Dazeley.

All other photographs are Peter Dazeley/Orbis
Publishing.